To Keith

Happy Cooking

You Old Bastard!

A Lifetime on the Stove

Jonathan Fraser

Edited by
Hannah Fraser

Designed by
Sophie Congdon

Published in Great Britain in 2018 by The Independent Publishing Network for
The Hat and The Mouse
34 Connaught Avenue,
Frinton-on-Sea,
Essex,
CO13 9PR

Copyright © Jonathan Fraser, 2018

All rights reserved.

No part of this publication may be reproduced, stored or transmitted in any form by any means, electronic, mechanical, photocopying or otherwise, without the written permission of the publisher (The Independent Publishing Network).

The right of Jonathan Fraser to be identified as Author of this work has been asserted by them in accordance with the Copyright, Designs and Patents Act, 1988.

Hardback ISBN: 978-1-78926-873-7
eBook ISBN: 978-1-83853-020-4

For Moto, Peapod, Bisty and Dids

Contents

Introduction: A Lifetime on the Stove 7
The Story behind The Hat and the Mouse 9
Savoury 15
The Easiest Ruby in the World 19
Cazalis – The Turning Point 23
Eggs 25
Another Cookery Book 27
Bread 29
Gluten-Free 33
Jacob: Baking in the Bush 35
Cheese Scones 37
Under Wraps 39
Salad Dressing: There's nothing like being well dressed!. 41
Eric: A Chef's Tale 43
Quick Quick Slow Duck 45
Paprika Goulash: The Sweet Spice of Life 47
Sweet 49
Sort it out! 61
Fatboys: Potato and Chocolate? Sounds Disgusting! 63
Bisty's Fudge 65
The Original Sticky Toffee 67
The Case of the Lemon Tealeaf 69
Wipers Time Cake 73
Das ist ein großer Apfelstrudel 75
Night and Day (Dark and White Chocolate Truffle Cake) 79
Profiteroles: The Taming of the Choux! 81
Chicago Charlie 83
Nuts: Are you NUTS about Nuts? 85
Phew! How Many Eggs? 87
Sweet Success 89
Simple Biscuits 91
Scone Secrets 93
Handlebar Herbert 97
Ice Cream 99
Meringues: It's all Air, Sugar and Cream! 101
No Mousse at The Mouse 105
Magic Hands Holgate 107
Scrumping Time 109
A Tart Tart 111
What a lovely Pear! 113
Roger Roger, le Dodger 115
Christmas 117
Christmas Tips 119
The Gravy 121
You must be baking mad! 123
Icing a Cake 125
Festive Feasting – Mince Pies! 127
Festive Feasting Continued… 129
Chocolate Truffles 131
Bermuda Tea 133

A Lifetime on the Stove

It is akin to performing on the piano. This is how one might describe stove cooking during À La Carte service, whether on an exclusive French range like Charvet, or a simple domestic hob. Pans are shifted, tossed, whisked and stirred with such ferocity that it is comparable to a classical pianist! Chefs get a buzz from this as adrenalin pumps through the veins!

I was classically trained in French cuisine from a very young age. I started in professional kitchens on my fourteenth birthday. At sixteen, I entered my first competition – the Junior Omelette Class at the *Hotel Olympia*. To my mother's despair, I was using dozens of eggs every day, practising flat and folded omelettes as well as the difficult Baverse jam omelette.

The French explanation of the omelette is rather fanciful. It is claimed that a Spanish King lost his way in the forest while on a journey. Being ravenous, he entreated a peasant he encountered to rustle up some grub quickly for him and his entourage. The humble subject speedily whipped up a superb omelette. This strange dish was totally nouvelle cuisine to the ruler. The King was so impressed by the deft way the skillet was handled, the King exclaimed: "Quel homme leste (What an agile man)!" 'Homme leste' then evolved into the term omelette. (As also told by Pierre Larousse in *Gastronomique*).

Having had an extensive career travelling around the world, I have worked in some of the best kitchens, from small restaurants to large banquets in 5-star hotels.

I must admit that the best meal I ever had was in Italy, at a small restaurant in Limone Sul Garda, with a small party of Michelin-starred chefs. The 'Chef Patron', Massimo, cooked us Tagliatelle with Asparagus. It was so simple but perfect. Since then, my philosophy has been that "No matter whether it's a sandwich, scone, Yorkshire pudding, or an omelette – make it the best".

The Queen's Silver Jubilee Celebration Dinner (Summer, 1977).
(JF in the middle, learning from the top Michelin-starred French Chefs).

The Story Behind

My wife Jasmine and I opened Frinton's food venue, *The Hat and The Mouse*, in the heart of Connaught Avenue in August 2011. We returned to our home county of Essex, having spent over 20 years working in and around the city of Bath.

I am well known in the 'Chef' world and I have worked alongside many celebrity chefs during my career, which has taken me all over the world. I trained in Southend-on-Sea, then on to London's West End and across the globe in America, Europe, Asia and Africa. I have also cooked for royalty and stars such as Cary Grant, Frank Sinatra and Alec Guinness.

I was a member of the National Culinary Team, winning medals and trophies in all areas of culinary work. I have appeared on my own television series and have been commissioned by Mercedes, Silver Spoon and Cadbury's.

Our first small business was *FoodArt* where the bread mouse was born – a very long-tailed mouse made from leftover bread dough. They became so popular in Bath that Jasmine, my wife, designed a logo of a 'Toque' (a chef's hat) and two mice – representing our two daughters. *The Hat and The Mouse* is a play on words. I'm constantly getting post and invoices to The Cat and The Hat or The Hat and The Cat, which I suppose is to be expected.

We live in Clacton-on-Sea and are delighted to be back on the coast. Our plan was to return the business to days of the 'Wallis Patisserie'. Mr Michael has already paid us a visit and endorsed the current standard of food being produced.

I told him that my father was a wedding cake specialist. In 1966, during the World Cup, he would have me pipe out royal icing full roses and buds for his cakes whilst watching the footie! Most people buy cakes these days but I would like to find a young apprentice to pass on those skills.

In addition to this, I also discovered that I am connected to the 'Mouse man' carpenter, Mr R Thompson of Kilburn, Yorkshire – my uncle married his sister.

JF at Le Francais in Rosebank, Johannesburg

JF (third standing from the right) in the international culinary team with Billy Gallager – the world President of Chefs

2011, the opening year for The Hat and The Mouse

Three course fine dining #1

Three course fine dining #2

The Easiest Ruby in the World

Coriander must be the most popular herb ever! Think of Thai food, Mexican dishes (Cilantro), Indian curries and so on. You can use the whole herb as the stalks are not bitter, like others, which makes it cheaper and easier to use. This Thai green base can be used with chicken, prawns, monkfish, or lobster.

It keeps well in the fridge but it is not recommended for freezing. We also keep the paste gluten-free, vegan and dairy free which solves a lot of problems with today's tastes.

Ingredients for the sauce

- 1 large bunch of Coriander
- 2 cloves of Garlic – peeled
- 1 finger size piece of Ginger – peeled
- 1 can of good Coconut Milk (400ml)
- ½ a jar of Mango Chutney
- 4-5 Green Chillies – split and de-seeded
- A good shake of Soy Sauce

Ingredients for Thai Green Curry

- 3 Chicken Breasts
- ½ a pint of Double Cream
- ½ a can of Coconut Milk (200ml)
- A pinch of Salt (for seasoning)

Tip: (Thai basil, Shrimp Paste, Squid Sauce – add these for a more authentic Thai paste).

Note: A jug blender is required.

Method: The Sauce

1. Put all these ingredients in a jug blender and mix away to a smooth, green and creamy consistency.
2. You may have to stop and stir the mixture a couple of times to ensure the herbs are well mixed into the liquid.
3. Jar the mixture up and store it in the fridge.

Method: Thai Green Chicken (for four)

1. Put ½ a can of coconut milk (200ml) with ½ a pint of double cream in a large wide pan. Add 3 diced/cut up chicken breasts and season with salt.
2. Then add 6 tablespoons of the paste/sauce. Stir this in and set to boil at a fast pace, stirring every so often.
3. The sauce should reduce and thicken as the chicken cooks. Cook for 10 minutes or so. Check a couple of the chicken pieces to ensure that they are thoroughly cooked inside.
4. Add green vegetables like French beans, mange tout, runner beans and/or broccoli, which need to be pre-cooked and refreshed, or alternatively, add spinach, pak choi and even peas which can go into the mixture raw and be cooked in the sauce for a few minutes before serving up.
5. Add more paste to your required taste and accompany with plain or sticky rice, noodles or potatoes.

Maitre Chef Maurice Cazalis
Restaurant Henri iV

31-33 Rue du Soleil d'Or

28000 Chartres
France

Tel.
(37) 360155

Cazalis
The Turning Point

"Wow! These guys are good!" This was some 35 years ago. I was a mere Sous Chef in a flashy 5-star hotel in Johannesburg. A team of French chefs under the leadership of Maurice Cazalis were touring the land on a culinary trip. They were with us for one week and my job was to look after them, and basically, be their run around 'Commis Chef'.

Maurice, edging towards his 80s, was the 'patron' of the famous *Henri IV Restaurant* in Chartres (around an hour southwest of Paris). He had trained some of the world's leading chefs at that time, including Bodin, *L'hôtel de crillon à Paris* (Hitler's Parisian headquarters during the Second World War) and Marc Guebert.

Their professionalism, attention to detail and finesse greatly influenced and inspired me to follow in their footsteps. Consequently, I went on to work for Monsieur Guebert at *Le Francais* for two years and joined the International Culinary Team.

One dish that flew out every night was 'Sole de Douvres poele, champignon blanc en duxelles au gratin' – Whole Dover Sole with a white mushroom mousse and white wine sauce.

Here is a modern take on that recipe for the magic Beurre Blanc sauce which I use as a base for some of my fish dishes. This is a very popular sauce with our customers.

Fresh fish stock made from the bones of white fish such as turbot, sole, and brill are preferable but for this recipe, fish stock cubes can work just as well.

Reduction Ingredients
- 3 or 4 Shallots – peeled and sliced
- 2 cubes of Knorr Fish Bouillon Cubes
- ½ a pint of White Wine
- 1½ pints of Water

To finish
- ½ a pint of Double Cream
- 1 packet (250g) of Unsalted Butter (at room temperature)

Note: A jug blender is required

Method
1. Place the reduction ingredients in a large saucepan and set to boil at a fast pace.
2. Reduce by around half (10 minutes or so) then add the double cream.
3. Re-boil (careful not to boil over!) and reduce for a further 5 minutes until it reaches the consistency of thin cream.
4. Pour the mixture into a jug blender. Now, add the block of butter and fresh fish stock and then put on a slow speed to start, then switch to a faster one for just a few minutes. You can adjust the thickness by either adding a little water if too thick or more butter if too thin.
5. For that extra smooth finish, add a spoonful of lightly whipped cream just before serving, this acts as a good emulsifier.

Note: I have not added any seasoning. There is enough in the Bouillon!

Eggs

There is a strange myth about poaching eggs and all sorts of contraptions have been custom-designed to make the perfect poached egg. Well, in my opinion, having poached eggs all my life, it's all about the freshness of the eggs.

We get a weekly delivery of eggs and I always crack one to test the freshness and quality.

Tip: Crack the egg onto a plate, it should not run all over the surface, but the white should encircle and hold up the round yolk. If not, it means those birdies have not been fed correctly or they are old!

There are hundreds of egg recipes. One I remember is 'Oeuf en cocotte Cyrano de Bergerac'. An egg cooked in a ramekin dish with asparagus spears to represent Cyrano's nose! Another dish is Omelette Arnold Bennett made up of smoked haddock and cheese (from none other than *The Savoy*, of course).

Here is a recipe for Smoked Haddock and Chive Buck Rarebit that's great for lunch or dinner:

Ingredients

- 250-300g of Smoked Haddock
- 600ml of Milk
- 1 tablespoon of English Mustard
- A shake of Worcester Sauce
- A handful of Grated Mature Cheddar
- 2 Egg Yolks
- 100g of Plain Flour
- 4 slices of Thick Granary Bread (for toast)
- 4 VERY Fresh Eggs (malt vinegar to add)
- 100g of Unsalted Butter or Margarine

Method

1. Bring the haddock to the boil in the milk. Leave to cool a little. Take out the haddock and reserve.
2. Make a 'roux' with the butter and flour. Add the flavoured milk to make a thick béchamel.
3. Cook for 5-10 minutes in a thick bottomed pan (it will not burn or catch). Flavour as you wish with mustard, Worcester sauce, cheese and pepper etc., *(salt should not be required)*.
4. Transfer to a bowl and leave to cool. Stir in the egg yolks and add the chunky flakes of haddock.
5. Now, fill a saucepan with water and set to boil. Add a generous shake of vinegar to the water.
6. Toast the bread and set the grill on high heat. Butter the toast and spread on the haddock mix, then place under the grill.
7. Crack the eggs into four separate cups. Stir the boiling water and add the eggs one at a time.
8. After 2-3 minutes, remove with a slotted spoon and place on some kitchen paper.
9. When the rarebit is brown, place an egg on each slice. You can also cover the eggs with a little Hollandaise sauce.

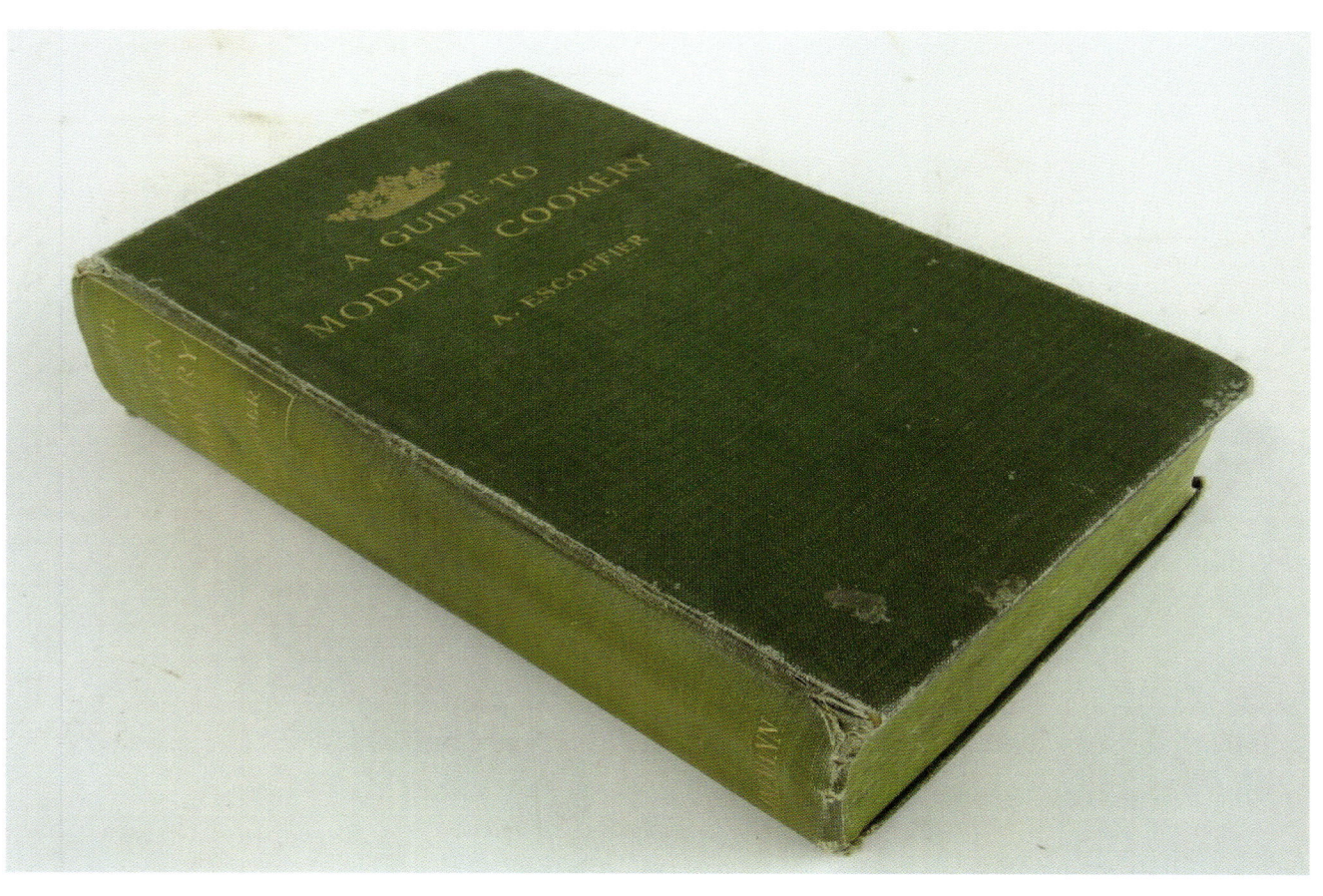

Another Cookery Book

Asparagus Ice, Oyster Soufflés, Blood Orange Hollandaise etc! Not trendy new recipes but from an old cookbook, known as the 'Bible', handed down to me from my Dad in 1973 – *A Guide to Modern Cookery*, by A. Escoffier (1908) – inscribed with 'SQMS Fraser G, HQ Rhine Army 1950'. Cookery books are best sellers on the book market and are often a must-have for the coffee table, but, if we're honest, we often just look at the pictures.

Back in those days, you could choose your type of caviar (Ossetra, Sevruga or Beluga). All menus were written in French as it was the language used in all the best cuisines. Catherine de' Medici is to blame as she brought her Italian Chefs to the French Courts thus inventing 'Haute Cuisine'. Today, a portion of caviar costs at least £160 plus 20% service at *The Savoy*, tea at *The Ritz* is £80 with a time limit, and a bottle of champagne on *The Orient Express* starts at around £125. Deep pockets are required!

But the age of style does not always mean high expense. Escoffier's book offers a holistic view of understanding cooking to produce high-quality end results by using the right cuts and ingredients.

It is often said that the sauce is the making of the dish. Dad would preach to me about the perfect Consommé and the fundamentals of good clear fond (stock). My very first lesson at college was on 'Fonds de Cuisine'. Today, folks seem to buy it all in, warm it up and smother it all over the food.

Anyway, enough now! Here are some golden rules for making stocks, soups, stews etc:

- Always use COLD water.
- Take off the foam/scum repeatedly, using a ladle, as it boils.
- Season the meat, fish, vegetables before you add the water when making soups, to release the flavour (osmosis).
- Simmer, or a 'ticking boil', don't furiously boil.
- Stir regularly to ensure even heat distribution.
- Meat – up to 4 hours, Poultry – 2 hours, Fish – 10 minutes (but leave to cool in the stock).
- *Note: Only when the bones are removed can the stock be vigorously boiled and reduced. Otherwise, the stock becomes bitter.*
- Stew, casseroles and curries always taste better the next day, but you need to cool the food quickly by transferring to a dish with a large surface area. These should really be refrigerated within 1.5 hours.

Bread

A bread making machine? Sure, if that's your preference, but why not try and make proper bread? We make our bread the traditional way, using fresh yeast, which is the by-product of brewing beer. *Marriages* is our local supplier who have been milling flour since 1824. The brown seedy (granary type) flour is the best I have ever used.

The first thing you'll need is fresh yeast. Ask the bakers behind the bread counter at your local supermarket. A kilogram block only costs around £2.00. Secondly, you'll need a very large bowl.

Here is a recipe for our brown bread:

Ingredients

- 1.5kg of Flour (1/3 of White Bread Flour and 2/3 of Granary Flour)
- 2 tablespoons of Salt
- 200-250g of Unsalted Butter or Margarine
- 75g of fresh Yeast
- 1 tablespoon of Sugar (any type)
- 2 cups of Water

Method

1. Preheat the oven on a low setting. Place 1.5kg of flour into a bowl (I recommend 1/3 of white bread flour and 2/3 of granary flour). Add in 2 tablespoons of salt and ½ a packet of unsalted butter or margarine.
2. In a separate bowl, weigh out 75g of fresh yeast with a tablespoon of any sugar.
3. Add 2 cups of tepid water (same as our body temperature – 37°C) to the yeast/sugar and slowly mix with a whisk. When diluted, add to the flour and start to make into a dough using one hand, adding more water as required. This will take some time but as the dough is formed, turn it out onto a floured table and continue to knead until smooth and elastic.
4. Place the dough in a separate buttered bowl, cover with a damp tea towel and place in the warm oven. Turn the oven off and place a tray of boiling water on the lower shelf forming a prover.
5. After 40-60 minutes, the dough should have doubled in size. If you have two ovens, turn the second one on to a high setting (200°C).
6. Turn out the dough onto a floured table and knead again to make a smooth dough. Cut, shape, egg-wash and seed (2-4 loaves), place these on greaseproof lined trays and return to the prover. Turn the oven on for a while and refresh the boiling water.
7. When the dough has doubled in size, carefully remove from the prover oven and place in the hot oven for 30-40 minutes, depending on size. You'll know when it's cooked by the appearance, smell and a hollow sound when tapped on the underside.
8. The more fat (butter/margarine/olive oil) that goes into the dough, the longer it stays fresh. For example, for brioche, this dough would need at least another 300g of butter plus 6 eggs!

Gluten-Free

Why is gluten-free (GF) so common now? Back in my day, no one knew of the term 'Coeliac', there were too many vegetarians! It seems to have somewhat become a trend that celebrities have adopted, influencing their fans and the media.

As a professional who works with flour every day, I have my own layman's theory…

It started when I began teaching twelve years ago. "You're making bread in this lesson, and you've got one hour", I was instructed. "Huh! How could we make loaves in such a short time?" I thought. Fast acting yeast was the answer. Mix the dough with the diluted yeast, mould, prove and cook. This was all wrong. It just did not look or smell like real bread.

'Normal' bread takes at least two hours to make, the dough has two proves and some doughs like Stollen and Panettone can have four, taking up to four hours to produce. Also, there are establishments that use an overnight dough where cold water is used and kept in the fridge to avoid over proving. This gives time for the gluten to thoroughly disperse and fully cook out. Fresh yeast, a product from ale making, gives the dough the aeration. Sourdough uses natural aeration which is fermented and kept for years. It is said that gluten intolerant folk are better off with this type of bread.

Of course, it was the Americans who gave us white flour with a high gluten quality, known as 'Strong Flour'. My miller tells me they are now producing flour with an even higher gluten strength, so they can add more water (more profits you see). Couple this with fast-acting yeast (now in liquid form) and this means that large bakers can produce more bread in less time and for less money. Worrying isn't it?!

Could this be why so many more people are suffering from the effects of undigested protein from flour in the stomach, thus causing irritation?

GF self-raising flour is 'okay'. The cake sponges are passable but not a patch on the real thing, but Scotch Pancakes often turn out well. However, pastry made from GF plain flour is another story. It is very short and crumbly, does not colour, and tastes awful. There are all sorts of recipes we are still trying out such as using coconut, rice, potato flours and Xanthan Gum.

However, ground almonds, although expensive, make great GF cakes. Like the Majorcan Orange and Almond Cake, Macaroons and Misérables. Try using GF digestive biscuits for cheesecake bases which can also be used as flan cases for Bakewell, Custard and Chocolate Tarts etc.

Jacob
Baking in the Bush

Grams and kilograms, pounds and ounces – totally unnecessary here! This was around 1980 in central Africa. A 5-star hotel in the middle of the 'Bush'. A brigade of 77 chefs catering for three restaurants and large banqueting suites.

Jacob Matakenya, like most Malawian folk, was christened after the Biblical name and was very genteel, polite and hard working. He had that little twinkle in his eyes that told you he just knew what he was doing. He had been a baker all his life and headed a team of six to make absolutely everything to do with bread in the hotel. The flour quality was just pot luck out there as there was no self-raising, soft, strong, fine ground or even spelt flour. What's more, the flour arrived in a large 50lb cloth bag (often torn).

Jacob would fill up the large mixer, plunge his hand in and feel it between his fingers. Then he proceeded to add the fat, yeast and liquid before forming it into the dough. A prover oven was not required as it was like working in a sauna, the dough would just prove so fast that extra hands were sent in to quickly mould the loaves, croissants, Danish pastries and yeast goods before baking.

The bread always came out the same – a nice crust, even texture and the right colour and aeration.

Working with Jacob was a joy. His hands worked the dough like magic. Perspiration soaked our thin cotton 'whites' and flour caked our shoes, but it was uplifting to see the final products coming out of the ovens.

We kept a carp farm for fish and had to provide feed for the chicken farmer. Five butchers were needed to joint down the 'whole' animals that arrived from who knows where! Another four chefs just to wash and prepare the vegetables. There was no ready-made mayonnaise, sauces and soups etc. We even made our own gelatine from animal feet. It was a holistic learning experience which now makes me laugh when I see our modern day professional kitchens.

Cheese Scones

The complexity of an English Scone

I have to say that it was only when we opened in 2011, that I had served scones for breakfast. Frinton folk are scone fanatics!

Here's a recipe for our cheese scones:

Ingredients

- 275g of Plain Flour
- 275g of Granary Flour
- 150g of Unsalted butter/Margarine
- 2 Eggs
- 1 teaspoon of Salt
- A pinch of Caraway seeds
- 150-200g of Cheese (strong Cheddar and a little Parmesan)
- 25g of Baking Powder
- 1 tablespoon of English Mustard
- A little dash of Milk (added last)

Topping

- A pinch of Rock Salt (for sprinkling)
- 1 Egg Yolk (for glazing)

Method

1. Mix all the ingredients together to form a smooth firm dough (but not dry). Leave the dough in the bowl, then cover and rest for 5 minutes.
2. On a floured table, pin and roll out the dough, turning as often as possible. It will spring back a bit due to the gluten in the granary flour. Aim for a ½-¾ inch thickness.
3. Now, use a very clean metal cutter (50-60mm), dipped into flour every so often to ensure a clean cut.
4. Line a baking tray with greaseproof paper and then place the scones out evenly on the baking tray.
5. Beat an egg yolk and brush only the tops. Place a small amount of cheese on each scone. Sprinkle with rock salt and let them rest for at least 20 minutes.
6. Bake in the oven at 160-170°C for around 15-20 minutes.
7. Now enjoy!

Under Wraps

We often hold 1-day cookery sessions on Sundays. It's very relaxed and social, everyone gets heavily involved in all sorts of food preparation. From fresh ravioli and bread, to duck and risottos.

"You actually cook it in the cling film? Won't it melt?" I am always asked this question. Well, did you know that 'Sous-vide', the trendy French cooking in a vacuum method, came about from using cling film? In particular, they found that foie gras (goose liver) can be lightly poached in consommé when heavily wrapped in cling film. Those of us who can remember duck a l'orange in a boil-in-the-bag will not be surprised! And of course, today, we can buy ready to roast chicken in a bag.

Salmon Fillet

For several decades, I have been cooking all sorts of food in such a manner. A large whole salmon fillet is an ideal way to get started. Try this method below instead of poaching a whole salmon in water (or a court-bouillion) whereby the fish can end up soft, wet, flavourless and very messy.

Method

1. First of all, pull off a large length of cling film and then lay the salmon fillet on top.
2. Season well with salt, pepper, a little olive oil and perhaps some herbs like basil, chives, coriander or chervil.
3. Fold over the cling film and repeat the process 3 or 4 times.
4. Lay the fish on a tray and bake in a preheated oven at 170°C for 25-30 minutes.
5. Check by pressing the centre and cook further for large fillets. Leave to cool on the tray and serve whole, decorated as you prefer with mayonnaise or lemon dressing.
6. The cling film will go hard but it will seal in all the flavours and keep the flesh moist and succulent.

Fillet of Beef

Bit of a secret this! But my Roast Beef Fillet is very similar.

Method

1. Take a trimmed whole fillet of beef (grass-fed if possible), this will be an expensive outlay of around £70 but it is worth it!
2. Draw out a large amount of cling film on the surface, sprinkle with lots of dried herbs of your choice.
3. Heavily season the beef on one side and lay that side on the film, now season again (beef fillet does not have the flavour of more muscular cuts so needs more flavouring).
4. Now, wrap and roll, then continue to roll with 8-10 layers of cling film. This also keeps the beef nice and round.
5. Pop it in a tray and ONLY cook in the oven for 30 minutes at 160°C. You may think I am mad but that's all you need!
6. Leave to cool for 20 minutes or so. Pierce the film as there will be lots of juices which can be used for the gravy/sauce.
7. If you really want it more well done, lay some slices on a tray and just pop it in the oven again. The meat is pink right the way through as opposed to well done on the outside and being very rare in the centre. It is soft, flavoursome and if done right, you will not even need a knife – it will 'cut like butter'.
8. For another time, try laying Parma Ham on the film first. Enjoy!

Salad Dressing
There's nothing like being well dressed!

"Never wear brown in town!" Well, never send out a salad undressed! It is a criminal offence in the chef world. Our modern life dictates us to buy all our ready-made dressings in a bottle. Aren't we getting lazy?! Yet, it's so simple to put together and will keep for ages.

Our basic salad leaf dressing uses olive pomace oil, which is a lighter version of olive oil made from crushed olives after pressing. It still contains all the high qualities but is milder in flavour and ideal for dressings. At college, we were taught a ratio of 1 vinegar to 3 oil, which is far too acidic for modern tastes. Nowadays, it's more like 1:6.

Basic Salad Dressing Tips:

In a large jug/bowl, measure in about half a litre of oil. Season with a tablespoon of table salt and a teaspoon of ground white pepper. Vigorously whisk in up to 100ml of white wine vinegar, drizzled in to form a cloudy appearance. That's it! Then just store in a bottle and remember to shake well before tossing into the salad. Rather than adding herbs, which the vinegar will 'kill', it is best to mix them with the leaves.

Caesar salad is another story. It's made using raw eggs (like mayonnaise) and must be kept refrigerated. Contrary to popular belief, the origins of the salad are not Roman. Various stories abound but it was made in Mexico from left-overs rustled together to feed American Pilots. The chef's name was Caesar Cardini.

Ingredients

- 500ml of Olive Pomace Oil
- 2 Eggs
- 1 small tin of Anchovies (not the fresh ones)
- 1 tablespoon of English Mustard
- A shake of Worcester Sauce
- A squeeze of Lemon Juice
- A shake of Tabasco Sauce
- 1-2 Garlic Cloves
- 4 tablespoons of Malt Vinegar
- Half a cup of Warm Water
- A little Salt and ground White Pepper (for seasoning)

Note: A jug blender is required

Method

1. Place ALL the ingredients, except the oil, into a jug blender and mix for 20 seconds.
2. With the blender on, slowly pour in the oil to form a mayonnaise-like texture.
3. Add more water to thin or more oil to thicken until you have the correct flavour and consistency. It's best to keep this in a sealed container in the fridge.
4. When making the salad, add grated parmesan and croutons to the salad (should be Romaine or Cos lettuce) and toss with the dressing.
5. Try it with Parma Ham baked crisp in the oven and strewn over the top.

The White Elephant Club on Curzon Street, Mayfair

Eric
A Chef's Tale

Nobody knew Eric's last name. His 'chef whites' were tatty, shoes caked in flour, syrup and all things sugary. In fact, you could call him a grumpy old so and so – barely a word left his mouth. His tiny pastry kitchen at *The White Elephant Club* on Curzon Street (Mayfair) was just like him – a disastrous mess!

This was in 1977. I was nineteen and had reached the heights of a 'Chef de Partie', responsible for the Larder section. It was in those days that a keg of lager was kept in the large cold-room just for the chefs (often at the start of the day!).

Eric would waddle through the kitchen mumbling and cursing at everyone and everything, but you dared not react so you just kept your head down. Even the 'great' Ronaldo, Maître d'hôtel, would even give him a wide berth. Nobody messed with Eric. But why?

Well, this chap, on his own, produced the most amazing pastry goods. Sugar pulling and blowing done the old fashioned way – on the open oven door and drawn through on a rather grubby old tea towel. *The Dorchester, Intercontinental* et al would ask him to make pieces such as pastillage, nougatines and cakes for their special clients.

On a couple of occasions in the evenings, when Eric was off work, a greasy waiter would be in a panic wanting a birthday cake for a celebrity guest (Joan Collins was one). "I'll do it", I would say. All the cakes were covered in Fondant, not an easy task. The next morning Eric exclaimed "Who made that cake", looking at the remains. "That was me, Eric, I didn't leave a mess did I?". "Huff" he replied.

As time went on, he would let me watch him and chat for a while. Tales of my Dad's career in the Catering Corp would go down well. Eric had three main things he cared about in life – his Irish Wolfhound (that loved all the turbot trimmings I squirreled away), his Renault 25 and his wife (and in that order!). He let on that he had worked on cruise ships, including the QE2.

You don't see true craftsmen like that today!

Quick Quick Slow Duck

There is no point dancing around the fact, duck is one of my favourite meals! Of course, back in the day, the leg was always served to the ladies as it is the best part of the bird.

Our first restaurant in Bath would sell up to 300 portions a week. It got a bit monotonous after a while but it is popular here in Frinton!

'Confit' is the correct term for cooking the duck (French, sorry about that!) Meat is cooked in duck or goose fat for a long time and can be kept sealed for a lengthy period in a larder, hence the recipe harks back to the time before the invention of refrigerators. Today, I see pulled pork on the menu in a lot of fast food eateries which is a version of confit called 'Rillette'. This is where the meat is heated and shredded with a fork.

When reheated and crispened, the duck becomes very tender and moist with a natural aromatic flavour. The oil is strained and stored (in the fridge) and re-used for the next time, or it can be used for crispy roasties.

This is a speedy recipe that does not involve overnight marinating.

Ingredients
- 2 packs of Gressingham duck legs (available in most supermarkets)
- 3 cloves of Garlic (unpeeled)
- 1 or ½ of Star Anise
- A good pinch of Salt
- 500ml-750ml of Vegetable Oil

Method
1. Take the four duck legs and using a large cooks knife, chop off the knuckles. Season with salt and place in a medium to large pan.
2. Add the star anise and garlic. Pour over the oil until the ducks are 'just' covered.
3. Bring to the boil and stir. Then place on a lid and simmer to a tick for around 2 hours. Stir occasionally to ensure even cooking.
4. Test by gently lifting a leg and pressing the flesh. It should be cooked through so that a piece of straw can be pushed through.
5. Leave to cool with the lid half on. At least 2 hours or so!
6. Take each duck leg by hand and twist the thigh bone to remove. Place the ducks in a tray for when required.
7. In a large frying pan, heat and place in the legs skin side down. Sizzle and brown to get them crisp. Now, put them in a hot oven for 15-20 minutes.
8. These can be served with salad, busy rice or sauté potatoes etc.

Paprika Goulash
The Sweet Spice of Life

It was not until I led a student culinary trip to Hungary that the awareness of paprika in everyday cooking became apparent. The markets in Budapest were strewn with an abundance of different types of this spice and the liberal use of it in so many national dishes is astonishing!

Before a hunt, a cauldron would be filled with diced meat (deer, beef or boar), onions, garlic, seasoning, a very generous amount of paprika, red wine, rosemary and caraway seeds. When the party returned hours later, the daube had turned into a rich flavoursome 'Goulash' eagerly devoured by the hungry hunters.

Whilst there, we visited a vineyard, which involved copious amounts of samplings and the owner's wife had prepared us all a meal. Yes, it was Goulash with just fresh bread. It was absolutely delicious, and the students tucked in with vigour whilst drinking even more red wine. A trip to remember!

Russian Stroganoff can often contain paprika (although the Queen has hers without), but with Goulash, it is the main flavour.

Here is our recipe using Beef Top Rump or Knuckle which I find the best cut for casseroles as it has good fat marbling, giving moisture and tenderness to the meat. I was always taught that you needed the same weight of onions to meat so do not be alarmed. This flavours and thickens the stew (so it's also gluten-free!). You can also add potatoes at the end.

Ingredients

- 1kg of large diced Beef
- 1kg of diced Onions
- A little Beef Stock
- 3 tablespoons of Sweet Paprika
- A pinch of Salt
- 1 or 2 sprigs of Rosemary
- 2 cloves of Chopped Garlic
- 1 whole tube of Tomato Purée
- A few Caraway Seeds
- Half a bottle of Red Wine

Method

1. Fry off the beef in a large pan with a little oil for 5-10 minutes. Season with salt and rosemary.
2. Add the onions and garlic and then continue to cook out for a further 10-15 minutes.
3. Now, add the tomato purée. Stir well and cook for 2-3 minutes. Strew on the paprika and stir in.
4. Add the red wine, then stir and boil.
5. As the casserole boils, use a ladle to remove the foam/scum from the top.
6. Taste the stock to check the seasoning and adjust accordingly.
7. Turn down the stock to a slow boil. It usually takes 2-3 hours to cook. Stir/remove the foam/scum regularly.
8. Like most stews, it will taste better when it has cooled down, or even the next day.
9. You can serve with bread, mash, noodles, or dumplings etc. Enjoy!

Surrealism in chocolate

Blown sugar

The counter at The Hat and The Mouse

The classic Banana Split

Bear chocolate

Chocolate art

Death by chocolate

Marzipan work

Forbidden Iced Parfait

Dalinian Inspired Coffee

Sort it out!

Late into Friday afternoon: "Finkleman's on the phone for you Jonathan". "How long will it take you to get here? We're at the *Langham*", Finkleman demanded.

A hasty hour later, I walked through the doors of the 'soon to be open' *Langham Hilton*. A £90m refurbishment of the old BBC building in the heart of London. After being pulled around by all sorts of Company Directors, I got into the kitchen to begin the arduous task of fixing the problems. "Bring in Jonny Whiz, he'll get it done". Princess Diana and Fergie were officially opening the hotel on Monday, along with hosting dinners for visiting overseas royalty. Now there was a challenge!

The Executive Chef had developed a nervous twitch on his left side and the housekeeper was in the hospital recovering from a nervous breakdown. Chaos ran through the building like blood in the veins. Chefs were hardly able to stand, they were so tired from supreme efforts to reach the highest standards of cuisine required.

By the next morning, 17 more chefs arrived along with box after box of equipment including trays, pans, utensils and storage containers. Selected supplier's vans pulled up with fully prepared fresh vegetables, meat cuts to specific specifications and fish all filleted, trimmed and portioned. The caviar trolley with Beluga, Sevruga and Ossetra needed proper blinis and accompaniments for the Russian cured salmon along with the 40 types of vodka.

We lost a few chefs on the way (including the twitching one), but by the end of the week, it became a smoother operation. When a hotel or restaurant opens, it has got to be all guns blazing. "You never get a second chance to make a first impression!". With lobsters alone, we got through 100 a day.

The German Hotel Manager swaggered around enjoying all the praise from guests and started to get some colour back in his cheeks.

Finkleman phoned back the following week, "Is it sorted?". "Well, Michael, I spent quite a lot", I replied.

"Yeah, is it sorted?" He retorted. "I've spent £140K", I uttered nervously. No response. "Yes, everything is okay now", I stated.

"Right, get yourself back to Head Office. Glasgow opens in three weeks".

Fatboys

Potato and Chocolate? Sounds Disgusting!

The things people put in cake these days. There's carrot cake, of course, courgette cake, beetroot cake (red velvet), to name but a few.

This recipe comes from a veteran Scottish Pastry Chef way back in the 1980s, when Sticky Toffee Pudding was the new exciting English dessert. Wayne was an excellent pastry chef. I employed him for the newly opened *Royal Berkshire Hotel* in Ascot, Hilton's Flagship Country House hotel. He had a repertoire of lovely old recipes and this is one that became a huge favourite. In fact, I still use this sponge today for most chocolate sponge cakes and gâteaux. The mashed potato gives it a wonderful texture.

Ingredients and utensils

Fatboy Sponges 2 x 8-9" tins, greased and lined with parchment paper

Bowl 1:
- 125g of Soft Margarine
- 150g of Caster Sugar
- 5 Egg yolks

Bowl 2:
- 150g of Self-Raising Flour
- 40g of Dark Cocoa Powder
- 15g of Bicarbonate of Soda

Bowl 3:
- 100g of Mashed Potato
- 75g of Dark Chocolate (pistils or broken into small pieces)

Electric Mix bowl:
- 5 Egg whites

Saucepan:
- 110g of Caster Sugar diluted with 3-4 tablespoons of Water

Method

1. Put the mash in the microwave for 1-2 minutes. Spatula in the chocolate which will melt into a smooth thick paste.
2. Cream the margarine/sugar/egg yolks together. Sieve in the flour and cocoa powder, and then fold into a batter. Then beat in the chocolate/potato paste.
3. Set the saucepan of diluted sugar to boil and put the egg whites in the electric mixer with the whisk attachment – do not turn on yet!
4. When the sugar syrup is boiling, turn on the mixer to the highest setting. After 1-2 minutes, when the egg whites are light and white, take the saucepan and slowly pour the syrup into the egg whites, whisking all the while. This is called Italian Meringue. Continue for another few minutes until thick.
5. Vigorously fold the meringue into the chocolate cake mix, divide into the prepared tins and bake at 150-160°C (fan) for 40-50 minutes. Test the centre to ensure it is cooked through.
6. Take this out of the oven and ensure you cool before turning out.

This is also great as a hot pudding with chocolate fudge sauce.

Bisty's Fudge

This is a bit of a secret recipe that I do not often share. My youngest daughter (nicknamed Bisty in our family) has a very sweet tooth. As a toddler, she would come into the hotel kitchen to see her Dad. Of course, I would spoil her with white chocolate mice and slithers of vanilla fudge, much to the dismay of her mother! Pristine clothes ruined with sweet delights.

Personally, I hate folded fudge which becomes crystallised. This recipe was developed from Mary Berry's niece, Amanda, who was being trained at the hotel. Amanda gave us the *Good Housekeeping* magazine with her Auntie's recipe. Obviously, we had to adapt it greatly as using cups and knobs is not applicable for larger amounts in a professional kitchen.

The fudge is finished with white chocolate which makes it smooth. When you think about it, white chocolate is merely reduced condensed milk with cocoa butter.

This will make an 8" x 6" tray and will keep for ages. You can make lots of variants from this basic recipe like whole hazelnut, coffee and walnut or even a Christmas version.

You will need a THICK bottom pan (preferably aluminium), otherwise, it will burn!

Ingredients

- 650ml of Cream (½ Whipping and ½ Double)
- 650g of Caster Sugar
- 200ml of Liquid Glucose
- A splash of Vanilla Essence or 1 split Vanilla Pod
- 200g of Unsalted Butter
- 200g of White Chocolate

Method

1. Put all the ingredients (cream, caster sugar, vanilla essence/pod and liquid glucose) in the pan, then stir with a thick whisk and set to boil on a fast flame/high heat.
2. Check and stir often. Boil for 20-30 minutes until you achieve the desired colour and texture. Your nose will tell you!
3. Meanwhile, melt 200g of unsalted butter in a glass jug in the microwave. Then melt 200g of white chocolate in a plastic bowl in the microwave for 30-second intervals. Ensure this is ready before the fudge is cooked, along with preparing a greaseproof lined tray to set the fudge.
4. Take the fudge pan off the heat, ladle in the top part of the melted butter (clarified), not the buttermilk residue at the bottom. Carefully whisk in 'til smooth.
5. Lastly, add in the melted white chocolate and immediately whisk. It will thicken quickly. Pour into the tray and leave to set until cold.
6. Cut, slice or cube up. You can also coat it in milk or dark chocolate.

Enjoy!

The Original Sticky Toffee

Ruth and Steve came from the *Lygon Arms* in Broadway. It was the mid-80s and upon returning from Chicago, the next mission was to open one of Hilton's Flagship hotels in Ascot. A beautiful setting backing onto Windsor Park's polo field. We were going full steam for Michelin-star recognition and set up innovating dining concepts. Would you believe I had to convince Robin, the General Manager, to write the menus in English as up until then, all the luxury country house hotels were still writing them in classical French?!

In addition, I would only use British cheese. Not the French ones, ours were much better I argued. I would buy whole Landes Ducks (not allowed today) and removed the beautiful pink foie gras. Then I proceeded to make four different preparations from the birds. We also got through a lot of caviar, my favourite of the three being Sevruga, which was used on numerous dishes such as fresh langoustine ravioli.

These two were fantastic enthusiastic workers and would often sneak back into the kitchen after I left to carry on preparing. One day, Ruth pulled out a tired old recipe sheet which came from the *Lygon's* Pastry Chef. He had worked at *Sharrow Bay* in the Lake District. It was Sticky Toffee Pudding. "What's that?" I asked. The rest is history.

Ingredients

- 6 Medium Sized Eggs
- 500g of Self-Raising Flour
- 650ml of Water
- 500g of Chopped Dates
- 3 teaspoons of Bicarbonate of Soda
- 175g of Unsalted Butter
- 500g of Dark Soft Brown Sugar
- ½ a teaspoon of Vanilla Essence

Sauce Ingredients

- 1kg of Dark Soft Brown Sugar
- 400g of Unsalted Butter
- ½ a teaspoon of Vanilla Essence
- 200ml of Double Cream

Method

1. Pre-line the cake tin with butter greaseproof/silicone paper.
2. Place 500g of chopped dates with 650ml of water in a large pan to boil.
3. Remove from the heat and whisk in 3 teaspoons of bicarbonate of soda. It will smell awful. Leave to one side to cool a little.
4. In a machine, cream together 175g of unsalted butter, 500g of dark soft brown sugar and ½ a teaspoon of vanilla essence until the mixture has a light and smooth texture. .
5. Add the 6 eggs and continue to mix in the machine.
6. Sieve and add the flour.
7. Mix again until smooth.
8. Then add the date mixture and continue to mix.
9. Pour into the prepared tin and bake at 160°C (fan) for up to 50 minutes until the cake has risen and is equally firm to touch all over.
10. Meanwhile, make the sauce.
11. In a thick bottom pan, set to boil on a medium heat/flame: 1kg of dark soft brown sugar, 400g of unsalted butter, ½ a teaspoon of vanilla essence and 200ml of double cream. Make sure to stir/whisk often.
12. If using straight away, cover the hot pudding with sauce and return to the oven to soak in.
13. If serving cold, cool down the sauce until it has a thick consistency. Coat all over and decorate.

The Case of the Lemon Tealeaf

You never think it will happen to you! It was during February half-term. 3.30am, when the workday begins, I noticed the back window open ajar. "Did I forget to close that last night?" I thought. I opened the door furtively and went through our restaurant, checking to see if anything was missing, disturbed or damaged. Nothing seemed amiss. The large knives were still on the work table and the charity tin still rattled with change. "Must get on", I thought.

A couple of hours later, our apprentice at the time, started to put signs out for the cakes in the counter. "Lemon Drizzle?", he asked. "Yes, it is amongst the others on the table", I replied.

Alas, it had gone! A 10-inch complete cake, iced and ready. The Walton-on-the-Naze Bobby who turned up later that day was sympathetic, but felt it was unnecessary to involve the likes of Sherlock Holmes!

So, for the 'Faganites' who stole the cake, here is the recipe should you ever decide to make one yourself:

Ingredients

- 5 Eggs
- 250g of Soft Margarine/Butter
- 250g of Caster Sugar
- 250g of Self-Raising Flour
- 3 large unwaxed Lemons
- 4 large tablespoons of Icing Sugar
- Royal Icing to decorate

Method

1. Grease and line with paper an 8 or 9-inch caked tin. Pre-heat the oven to 155°C.
2. Place a bowl on the scales and crack in the 5 eggs. They should approximately weigh 250g in total (50g for each egg).
3. Weigh the same quantity of margarine/butter and sugar together in a mixer bowl. Grate the zest of the 2 lemons, making sure that only the yellow rind is used – not the white pith (which is bitter).
4. Cream on the machine, or by hand using a spatula, until light and fluffy. Whisk in the eggs gradually.
5. Sieve in the flour (it is very important to aerate the flour).
6. Mix to make a smooth batter and spoon into the lined cake tin. Then smooth the mixture to an even level.
7. Bake at 155°C slowly for as long as it takes! 40 minutes or an hour. It all depends on the size and the type of oven. You will know when it's cooked by checking to see if it has come away from the side a little and the centre springs back.
8. Place on a wire rack and turn over after 5 minutes of cooling.
9. Now, squeeze the lemons into a small pan, add the icing sugar and set to boil. Give it a good fast boil for 1 minute, then, using a pastry brush, drench the cake with the mixture over and over.
10. Leave to cool and decorate accordingly, but as a precaution, take a photo before someone steals it!

Wipers Time Cake

It is a privilege every year to make a large boozy rich fruit cake for our local Royal British Legion. Laced with the tipple from Flanders Field in Belgium.

Here is the recipe adapted from a Christmas fruit cake. For me, moisture is key to a good cake so I use 50% oil with butter, cook on a low heat and feed the cake for several months. When marzipanning, go for a final dousing with alcohol helped with skewering deep holes, for the liquid to be absorbed.

Tip: The correct amount of marzipan should weigh a 1/3 of the cake weight! Pre-line the tin with buttered greaseproof/silicone paper.

This recipe is for a 10-inch square cake.

Ingredients

- 350g of Plain Flour
- 200g of Self-Raising Flour
- 3 tablespoons of Cocoa Powder
- 100g of Nibbed/Chopped Nuts
- 150g of Chopped Glacé Cherries
- 100g of Mixed Peel
- 250ml of Vegetable Oil
- 250g of Unsalted Butter/Margarine
- 250g of Caster Sugar
- 250g of Dark Soft Brown Sugar
- 4 tablespoons of Treacle/Molasses
- Flavours – Vanilla Essence/Almond Essence/Rum Essence/Mixed Spice
- 10 Medium Eggs
- A splash of Brandy or Rum and Wipers Time
- 2.5kg of Dried Mixed Fruit

Method

1. Place 2.5kg of dried mixed fruit in a large bowl and douse with brandy/rum and Wipers Time.
2. In a mixer, cream together the following ingredients: 250g of vegetable oil, 250g of unsalted butter/margarine, 250g of caster sugar, 250g of dark soft brown sugar, 4 tablespoons of treacle/molasses, then add a little of the following flavours – vanilla essence/almond essence/rum essence/mixed spice. Mix until light and smooth.
3. Then add 10 medium eggs and continue to mix.
4. Then add the following ingredients carefully and continue to mix: 350g of plain flour, 200g of self-raising flour, 3 tablespoons of cocoa powder, 100g of nibbed/chopped nuts, 150g of chopped glacé cherries and 100g of mixed peel.
5. After these are all well mixed, add the mixture to the fruit in the large bowl and thoroughly mix. Have a little taste and adjust if necessary!
6. Place into the tin and flatten down with wet hands or use a spoon.
7. Bake in a preheated oven set at 150-160°C for around 1 hour, then turn the temperature down to 130°C and continue to bake for a further 2-3 hours. Keep checking to ensure the cake does not over-colour by turning it around every so often for an even bake.
8. To be sure it is cooked, place a metal skewer right in the centre. Test the tip heat on your lips and see that the skewer is clean. Also, press around the edges and centre for firmness by ensuring it springs back to shape.
9. For storage, keep on a cake board wrapped in a plastic bag. Feed (sprinkle with booze) every week. The cake will soften and keep moist.
10. I have tried to write '*Remember*' in red icing on the cake, but my hands start to shake, it's too emotive.

Das ist ein großer Apfelstrudel

Walter Haiser owned the restaurant *The Old Vienna*. He was one of those large, bald, rotund and very smiley Austrians who was always cheerful and munching on something! He used both English and German in the same sentences so it took a while to understand him. He worshipped Russ the accordion player (he was the local postman from Basildon, but played a mean Eins Zwei G'Suffa).

1973 – Black Forest Gâteau, Prawn Cocktail, Wiener Schnitzel, Chicken Kiev, Baked Alaska, Duck à l'orange and Chateaubriand. These were trendy dishes back then – how times have changed?

Apple Strudel is a bit tricky to make, the pastry should be so thin that a newspaper can be read through it – like tracing paper. You also need an old tablecloth or a large apron to roll and pull out the pastry. We only really know of Apple Strudel but once I had to make one filled with red onion and lung (Lungenstrudel), not my favourite!

Needless to say, Walter ate lots of the apple cake and proceeded to teach me the real Austrian version that he had grown up with.

Ingredients

- 1kg of Plain Flour
- 5 eggs
- 2 tablespoons of White Wine Vinegar
- 10 Bramley Apples
- A pinch of Salt
- ½ a cup of Vegetable Oil
- 150g of Unsalted Butter
- 200-300g of Caster Sugar
- Cinnamon
- Mixed Spice
- Mixed Peel
- Mixed Fruit
- Flaked Almonds
- Icing Sugar (for dusting)
- Ground Almonds (for decorating)

Method

1. In a large bowl, add 1kg of plain flour, 5 eggs, 2 tablespoons of white wine vinegar, a pinch of salt and ½ a cup of vegetable oil.
2. Using only 1 hand, start to mix to create a soft elastic dough, adding a little water along the way.
3. When soft and smooth, mix it for 5 minutes to strengthen the gluten. You can clean your hands by dipping it in flour and rubbing both hands together.
4. Form into a flat ball, dredge a little more oil over all the surface and cover with 2 layers of cling wrap.
5. Depending on size, take 10 Bramley apples and peel, quarter and thinly slice them.
6. Place in another large bowl. Then add cinnamon, mixed spice, mixed peel, mixed fruit and flaked almonds. Toss over to mix in (do not sweeten with caster sugar yet).
7. Lay out the tablecloth on a large table and heavily dust with plain flour.
8. Mix the dough again and flatten to a round disc.
9. Flour again and start to roll out on the cloth. It will be very springy so only try to make it double the size, then cover over and rest. Meanwhile, melt 150g of unsalted butter in a glass jug.
10. Continue several times to roll and relax until the dough is half as large as the cloth.
11. After a rest, take the dough from underneath and pull out gently using the backs of the hands. Start to pull out each side. Then again, rest the dough until it can be pulled very thinly overlapping the cloth.
12. Brush the melted butter over the pastry dough, being careful not to make any holes. On the top third, sprinkle with ground almonds.
13. Add the caster sugar, to your taste, to the apples, then toss and strew over the ground almond section.
14. Trim off the top edges where it will be thicker, lift the cloth top end and start to tightly roll the apples forming a strudel.
15. Trim the other end pastry edge and continue to roll. The last part is where the flakiness comes from as the layers of pastry and butter form a lamination.
16. Transfer to a greaseproof/silicone lined tray. Brush all over with the remaining butter and bake at 180°C for up to 50 minutes, depending on the size.
17. When cool, dust with snow (icing sugar) and serve. Viel Glück!

Night and Day
(Dark and White Chocolate Truffle Cake)

There are many dos and don'ts in the culinary world. One of them is chocolate and gelatine. You should not need gelatine to set a chocolate mousse, the exception being for a chocolate Blancmange.

Here is a recipe for one of our favourite cakes that can be versatile for use as a dessert, on its own with coffee or an afternoon tea cake:

Why not put on a bit of Nat King Cole to get you in the mood!

Ingredients

Night
- 100ml of Whipping Cream
- 140g of Dark Chocolate (pistels or chopped)
- 250ml of Whipping Cream (you need two measurements)

Day
- 100ml of Double Cream
- 200g of White Chocolate (pistels or chopped)

Syrup:
- Flavour with either Vanilla, Brandy, Tia Maria, Grand Marnier and so on…
- 1 cup of Sugar (any type)
- 1 cup of Water

Chocolate Sponge: (made or bought in) cut into 2 thin layers. You will need a 'form', either round, square or oblong.

Method

1. Firstly, make the syrup by boiling the sugar and water together in a pan for around 30 seconds. Then lay the first sponge in the form to cover the base. Using a brush, soak the sponge with ½ of the hot syrup mixture.

2. Set the 100ml of whipping cream to boil in a large pan. Remove from the heat and add the chocolate pieces stirring with a spatula to make a 'ganache'. Now, whip the 250ml of whipping cream to a soft, medium peak. Carefully fold in the ganache and spread evenly over the sponge.

3. Lay on the other layer of sponge and heavily soak with the remaining syrup. Repeat the process with the white chocolate mix. Smooth over the top and set in the fridge/freezer.

4. To serve, remove the form and either dust with good quality cocoa powder or pour on another ganache made with 125ml of double cream, 100g of dark chocolate and a tablespoon of liquid glucose.

Profiteroles
The Taming of the Choux!

If you can make a good Yorkshire pudding, then you can easily make profiteroles, choux buns and eclairs. Aren't they almost the same? Like Yorkies, they need to be thoroughly cooked as they will deflate if not fully cooked inside. Some chefs freeze them which I find makes them a bit soggy and they can break easily when dipped in chocolate or hot sugar. This recipe is in 'old money' – the two numbers to remember are 4 and 5.

It's the filling that really makes a good bun. Those bought-in ones from the supermarkets seem to be filled with air and watery, milky, tasteless cream – a mistake methinks!

Fillings:

- Fresh Cream – Whip 1-pint of Double Cream, ½ a pint of Whipping Cream, a cap of Vanilla Essence and a little Icing Sugar.
- Diplomat Cream – ½ Crème Pâtissière and ½ Fresh Cream.
- A good tip when filling is to make a hole in the base with a clean and empty biro pen case before piping.

Toppings:

- For Profiteroles – Boil 200ml of Double Cream, remove from heat and add 200g of Milk Chocolate. Stir with a spatula until smooth and leave to cool.
- For Eclairs and Choux – Fondant or Royal Icing (with a touch of Glycerine) flavoured with very strong diluted Coffee.
- For Chocolate – Boil 150ml of Double Cream, remove from heat and add 180g of Dark Chocolate and a tablespoon of Liquid Glucose.
- To make a Croquembouche (crack in the mouth), it should be filled with a liqueur flavour, use Diplomat Cream and dipped in very hot sugar syrup. This one needs a lot of taming!

Method

1. Put a ½ a pint of cold water in a good saucepan (thick base if possible), then add 113g of unsalted butter or margarine. Weigh up 142g of strong bread flour in a separate bowl.
2. Set the water and butter to boil on slow heat. When the butter has melted, turn up to boil. Take off the heat, add the flour and beat vigorously to a smooth paste. Return to the heat, stirring all the while for 3-5 minutes until the mixture becomes a smooth dough leaving the pan clean.
3. Transfer to a mixing bowl and beat in 4 or 5 eggs, one at a time. After adding 4 eggs, the mixture should 'just' fall from a wooden spoon/spatula. Scoop the mixture into a piping bag and pipe onto a tray with silicone/greaseproof paper. This makes about 8 good sized eclairs or 25 choux buns.
4. Bake at 170°C (fan) for 25-30 minutes then turn down at 150°C and continue to bake for a further 20-30 minutes. Just because they have risen does not mean they are cooked inside. Don't be impatient! Take out the oven and leave to cool on the tray.

Chicago Charlie

Everyone loved Charlie, the 5ft 2" African American Banquet Chef of the largest *Ramada Hotel* in the world.

I first met Charlie three decades ago when I took on the challenge of seeing through a total refurbishment of a big airport hotel. Being in my fearless mid-twenties, I needed all the help I could get. The daily functions catered for up to 3,000 people in 85 different rooms. Charlie was indeed the 'Main Man'. He was forever cheerful, talked far too much and just took everything in his stride. Roasting 120 whole fillets of beef, searing 650 chicken escalopes for teriyaki, 800 house salads and it went on.

His sidekick, nicknamed 'Shoes' (because of his very large feet!), was the Head KP (kitchen porter) who gathered together all the equipment ready for Charlie. Together, they made a formidable team.

We had a special function coming up, so I brought over an English colleague who was really into all 'Michelin-Star' stuff and was a bit arrogant when it came to food. Dicky had been my Sous Chef, so he knew the standards I expected. "Go and spend your first day with Charlie", I said.

Dicky had looked around and seen the food plates going out and huffed a bit, pooh-poohing the quality. After an hour, I went to see how he was getting on. Charlie had him piping the seasoned hot mash onto jacket potato skins. 700 were needed. Beads of sweat were pouring from his forehead and the veins in his right arm were about to burst. I chuckled inside, he had only finished 25! Charlie took over and completed the rest in 10 minutes. After that, Dicky kept quiet.

At the end of the week, he realised just how much food was produced at a consistently high standard. Hence, Charlie was elevated to a culinary God!

We had a Marshal Michleby oven (British, of course), that had seven rotating shelves. Each shelf was the size of a single bed. There were 13 switches to get it going. It cost almost $10,000 just to move it to another part of the kitchen during the renovation. It had approximately 2,500 baking sheets stacked floor to ceiling. On a busy day, you couldn't get your hands on one!

Nuts
Are you NUTS about Nuts?

Can we blame Frank Muir? Those whole hazelnuts (or filberts) in a bar of chocolate could be the reason. "Everyone's a fruit and nut case!". Did you know ground or flaked almonds are free of VAT? So are walnuts, pecans, desiccated coconuts, cashews, shelled hazelnuts and so on. But, when a hazelnut is peeled, it becomes subject to VAT. Nuts if you ask me!

Almonds are easily the most used nut in pastry kitchens, such as for marzipan, Florentines, frangipanes, cakes and biscuits etc. They are expensive and seem to increase in price as demand grows. Hence, I often find the supermarket products are bland and contain fewer nuts substituted by cheap flour.

Here is the recipe for our popular Bakewell Tart:

There are lots of versions but after six years, we must have made in excess of 500.

Ingredients

- 3 Eggs
- 155g of Soft Margarine
- 155g of Caster Sugar
- 120g of Ground Almonds
- 35g of Self-Raising Flour
- 1 tablespoon of Almond Essence
- A tablespoon of good Raspberry Jam (with seeds)
- 2 tablespoons of Royal Icing
- A splash of Lemon Juice
- Melted Chocolate (for decoration)
- A 7" pastry lined Fluted Tin

Method

1. Crack the eggs in a dish and weigh them, they should weight approx. 150g. Let's say they weigh 155g.
2. Weigh out 155g of soft margarine and 155g of caster sugar in a mixing bowl, add a tablespoon of almond essence and cream with a whisk/spatula.
3. Add the 3 eggs and continue mixing.
4. Take 35g of self-raising flour and 120g of ground almonds (this adds to the 155g) and fold into the mixture to create a smooth paste.
5. Spread a thin layer of raspberry jam on to the lined pastry tin and carefully dab on the almond mixture in small amounts to fill up the tin evenly.
6. Bake in the oven at 160°C for 30-40 minutes, making sure the base pastry is cooked (turn down the oven and cook for longer if necessary). Leave to cool for around 30 minutes.
7. To finish, take a couple of tablespoons of royal icing and dilute with lemon juice to a thick but self-levelling consistency.
8. Scoop on to the tart and spread to the edge (a step palette knife is best for this task).
9. Pipe a thin spiral of melted chocolate from the centre and, using a toothpick, feather a design of your choice by drawing through the icing/chocolate. Leave to set for a while.
10. This tart lasts for a long time as the almonds keep it moist. In fact, some customers prefer the taste after a few days.

Phew!
How Many Eggs?

Our eldest daughter Polly (Peapod), got married in 2015. There was the dress, the veil, the wine, the menu, the band, the champagne, the port, the car, the pianist, the photographer…and on it went relentlessly. Talk of nothing else entered the conversation, emails and phone calls etc. What about the cake?

Well, of course, I had to make it the best cake I had ever made, and Peapod is a chocoholic! Six sheet sponges each with 20 eggs, three vanilla Madeira sponges and three 'Fatboys' chocolate sponges. Six round tiers each with four layers cut out to make a harlequin 'battenberg' effect, held together with boiled apricot glaze, vanilla buttercream and chocolate ganache. The base tier was 14" in diameter, grading to a 5" top tier.

Now for the hard bit. Getting the timing just right. This was my cake plan/schedule before her big day!

Thursday – Make up 80 dark and white chocolate roses in 'plastic' chocolate (made using melted chocolate and glucose).

Friday – Coat each tier with boiled apricot jam, this will help the chocolate coating adhere and keep the sponges moist. Add the ganache coating made from 1.5 litres of cream, 1.4kg of milk and dark chocolate, and 150g of glucose.

When set, each tier was piped with tempered white chocolate dots all over the side. Around 350 dots per tier (I felt like Clarence the cross-eyed lion after that). The cakes were left in an air-controlled chiller until the morning. Knock up a chocolate butterfly, a mandatory mouse and a robin (for Peapod's Gran – she also loved chocolate).

Saturday – When to assemble? 9.00am, go for it! Five wood dowels in each tier. Make up the two three-tiered cakes, three for the bottom section and three for the top section. Arrange the chocolate roses around. Then make up a six-foot white and dark chocolate ribbon and bow to join the two cakes when we set up at the venue.

It was wonderful weather on the big day, but a bit too hot for chocolate. The cake stood up well and was eaten as the wedding breakfast dessert with a quenelle of Crème Chantilly. The next one should be easier as my other daughter is a lover of fresh strawberries and cream.

Sweet Success

Sugar hates humidity, so delay any ideas of icing and decorating cakes if you can! And your Brandy Snaps will flop in just a few hours. I made a Croquembouche for a wedding that was almost a disaster as the spun sugar (candy floss) started to wilt as we took it out of the air-conditioned car.

Sugar is just an amazing food. Cane or beet, its properties are endless and quite incredible. Anyone who has made a simple Crème Caramel or Nougat de Montélimar will have seen how it changes from syrup to 'Blackjack'. Edward Notter (trained by Delainey) is one of the world's most famous sugar artists. I spent a week with him in Zurich back in the 80s and the pieces he produced were just amazing – pulling and blowing huge fruit baskets, birds, animals and figurines etc. Next time you're in the South of France, it's worth going to *Yves Thuries Sugar Museum* in Carcassonne.

Facts and Tips

- The less refined sugar is best for boiling.
- For meringues – Use granulated sugar rather than caster sugar.
- Use icing sugar, or 50%, for sweet pastry. 100% for gluten-free pastry.
- Dark soft brown sugar needs to be warmed for cakes. Otherwise, lumps can stay in the sponge.
- Always add a little extra glycerine to royal icing to stop it going hard.
- Use sealed bags for regal icing/marzipan. Cling wrap is NOT airtight.
- Tate & Lyle sugar is the best (according to Notter!).
- Sweeten whipped cream with icing sugar (and vanilla – 'Chantilly').
- Dilute the sugar/water the day before. This stops it crystallising.

Simple Biscuits

This simple recipe for biscuits can be adapted to suit your tastes – experiment with different shapes and flavours.

Ingredients

- 900g of Plain Flour
- 600g of Unsalted Soft Butter or Margarine
- 150g of Caster Sugar
- 150g of Icing Sugar
- 1-2 caps of Vanilla Essence
- A pinch of Mixed Spice
- 5-10g of Sultanas (if required)
- Caster Sugar (sprinkling for decoration)
- Cherries or Nuts (for decoration)
- Royal Icing (for decoration)

Method

1. In a large bowl, place 900g of plain flour, 600 of unsalted soft butter or margarine, 150g of caster sugar, 150g of icing sugar, and a good splash of vanilla essence and a little touch of mixed spice. And perhaps a handful of sultanas?
2. Work this mixture into a dough, then roll into a long sausage – approximately 2-3" thick.
3. Wrap this in greaseproof paper and refrigerate for 1 hour or overnight. Slice and place the discs on paper, then bake in a preheated oven for 15-20 minutes at 170 180°C.
4. Sprinkle with lots of caster sugar as soon as they come out of the oven.
5. Decorate as you wish with royal icing, cherries, nuts etc.
6. These biscuits will go perfectly with a nice, strong cup of tea!

Scone Secrets

So you've had a go at the cheese scones, now do you fancy making some freshly baked scones, slathered with clotted cream and jam instead? But the question is, do you put the cream or jam on first? A great debate which still divides many across the UK!

Ingredients

Basic Recipe: (add dried fruit/sultanas/dates/vanilla if required).

This recipe makes 12-16 scones depending on size.

- 500g of Plain flour (or half Wholemeal/Granary)
- 125g of Unsalted Butter or Margarine
- 125g of Caster Sugar
- A pinch of Salt
- 20-25g of Baking Powder
- 2-3 Eggs
- A little Milk (to mix)
- Egg Yolk Wash (to glaze)

Method

1. Mix all the ingredients into a ball to form a smooth dough. Turn out onto the floured worktop and work for a short while until the dough is consistent. Leave for a minute or two.
2. Roll out to an even thickness of ½ inch and proceed to cut out the scones using a cutter/glass. Place onto a silicone lined baking tray. Re-work the leftover dough and repeat, resting the dough for 30 seconds before cutting out the scones.
3. Glaze with egg yolk wash, being particularly careful not to let the wash run over the sides.
4. REST for a least 15 minutes – this will stop them shrinking and looking like pyramids!
5. Bake at 180-190°C for 12-15 minutes. Leave to cool on the tray and they will continue to cook.
6. Split and layer with jam and cream. I spread the jam on first!

Handlebar Herbert

You know the type; blonde hair, athletic body, blue eyes...and the manicured bushy moustache. It was Christmas Day in 1972, my first day of work. Dad was in the larder section knocking up half a dozen 'Black Forests' while waiting for the Apple Strudels to finish off in the oven.

I was fourteen years old when I was first introduced to the world of 'Cuisine'. It was fast and exhilarating, everyone was rushing around, conscious of the clock ticking its way to the midday start of service. Hordes of folk would be arriving for their special treats. No time for too many niceties – "There's the pot wash sink, and the dishwasher is at the other end – stack and go! 8 strong teas with sugar when you have a moment lad!"

By the time I was sixteen, and with many lessons bunked off school to go to work, I was working alongside Herbert on the main courses. I could skin any animal, butcher down a haunch of veal in 9 minutes, skin live eels, turn 200 château potatoes in 25 minutes and easily produce 100 portions of Baked Alaska, ready for the flambé. It was the work ethic I admired the most. A bit like German cars I guess, efficient productivity with quality.

Herbert was a great teacher and well respected by all his staff. He loved fast cars and those stinking French cigarettes. His career included working in most of the grand hotels in Europe from the *George V* and *Hôtel de Crillon* in Paris to the *Hotel Sacher* in Vienna. He worked so hard, almost uniquely, had an English sense of humour! 'Cor Blimey' and 'Bloody Nora' in a German accent is quite funny! The laughter and banter created a brilliant atmosphere for a young lad to work in.

It was very 'classical' food, written in French such as Filet de Sole Véronique, Homard Thermidor, Tournedos Rossini, Chateaubriand, Entrecote Café de Paris etc. We still use French a lot these days, Crème Brûlée sounds much better than 'Burnt Cream' and a Jus gravy is preferable to a 'Juice' gravy.

After four years under Herbert's tuition, I flew through college and started working in the West End. I was able to take everything in my stride with confidence having learnt from a true master.

Picasso-inspired helados

Ice Cream

Honestly, the amount of kitchen gadgets you 'must have' is crazy! Most of them are at the back of a cupboard – the Pasta Machine, Bread Maker, Spiralizer, Egg Poacher, Juice Extractor etc…the list goes on. Can you remember, back in the 1980s, having to purchase a Whole Salmon Poaching Pan?

This is a recipe for an ice cream parfait. It has a smooth soft texture just like the ice cream they make in Italy – the home of Gelato.

Parfait means perfect. You can make all sorts of different flavours from this recipe, say the addition of liqueurs like Grand Marnier, Calvados or Malibu to name a few. This will produce around 8-10 portions and is served with chocolate sauce, Crème Chantilly and hazelnut meringues.

Ingredients

- 8 Egg Yolks & 2 Whole Eggs in a large glass or stainless steel bowl (10 Eggs in total)
- 225g of Caster Sugar
- 2 heaped tablespoons of Instant Coffee diluted with the smallest amount of Hot Water
- A shot of Tia Maria or Kahlúa
- 400ml of Double Cream – whipped

Method

1. Add the sugar, coffee and liqueur to the 10 eggs and whisk vigorously over a pan of simmering water for 5-10 minutes. A 'Balloon' whisk is favourable.
2. Then use either a hand electric whisk or mixer and continue to aerate (off the heat) until the mixture is thick, light and creamy (similar to sabayon otherwise known as zabaione).
3. 'Fold' in the whipped cream using the whisk again and place the mixture in a suitable tureen or container. Leave to freeze overnight. The combination of sugar and air means that the mixture will have the texture of soft scoop ice cream.
4. Why not try making different flavours and setting them in between layers of thin liqueur syrup soaked sponges? An ice cream gâteau. Yummy!

Meringues
It's all Air, Sugar and Cream!

Meringues! Yes, there are 3 main types – Traditional, Italian (boiled) and Swiss. To be honest, it's all about long whisking and lots of sugar. The Italians are the inventors of meringues, creating vast centre-pieces for impressive buffets.

The French, of course, have their own type which is poached in milk (Oeufs à la neige). The Scandinavians have their Baked Alaska. The Japanese have their nutty version (known as Japonaise no less!).

Right, let's get the rules set down. Firstly, cleanliness is paramount, clean the mixing bowl thoroughly. Some folk rub half a lemon inside the bowl to ensure there is no grease. Whisk the whites first to a peak and slowly add the sugar whilst whisking all the while. Cooking – for basic meringues/pavlovas, the cooking specifications are 1 hour at 100°C, I prefer a non-fan oven for this. Some recipes include cream of tartar or cornflour as a stabiliser (I don't). I prefer to use egg whites at room temperature, so if you have some left over from a Crème Brûlée or Hollandaise Sauce, take them out the fridge for a while.

Here is a recipe for piped meringues:
(This makes 12 good-sized rope shaped meringues).

Ingredients
- 150g of Egg Whites (from approx. 5 eggs)
- 250g of Granulated Sugar
- 60g of Roasted, Skinned and Crushed Hazelnuts
- 1 litre of Whipping Cream
- A pinch of Salt

Method
1. Set the egg whites to whisk in a mixer at full speed. Add a few grains of salt (my Dad's tip!). Whisk for 3-5 minutes until a firm peak is achieved. Then, SLOWLY start to add the sugar whilst whisking all the while.
2. Continue to whisk for 5-10 minutes, until the mixture is very firm. It will be noisy but keep the machine on until you are sure the mixture is fully peaked. Remove the whisk attachment and gently fold in the nuts with a large spatula. Fill up a piping bag (I prefer not to use a nozzle) and pipe out onto good silicone paper, making sure they are not too close together.
3. Bake at 100°C for 1 hour. After the hour, turn off the oven and leave the meringues in to dry out a little more.
4. When cool, sandwich together with 'Chantilly' cream and decorate with fruit and/or chocolate. For the Chantilly, try using half double and half whipping cream, good vanilla essence and icing sugar to sweeten. Whipping cream on its own tends to flop.
5. To make a Pavlova, use the same recipe, but you may need more meringue. The ratio of egg whites to sugar is 3:5, so 300g of egg whites and 500g of sugar. Omit the hazelnuts if required or alternatively, try adding coconut or nibbed almonds.

Mango and Hazelnut Japonaise – Pavlova

A Bevy of Swans

No Mousse at The Mouse

"Can't even make a bit of Choux Pastry". This is me shouting at the TV whilst watching yet another cookery show. Undercooked, misshaped and uneven eclairs and profiteroles. It's the BBC 2's 'Crème de la crème'.

Some of the skills are amazing and take years of practice to perfect, like pulling sugar into ribbons and flowers for example. Alas, the basics seem to be abandoned. Anything containing yeast seems to just flop.

This reminds me of a very prestigious competition in France called MOF (The Best Craftsman of France). It runs over a few days and the standard is truly incredible. The President awards the prize which includes a red, white and blue ribbon for the chef jacket. It is illegal to wear the ribbon without the actual award. As far as I am aware, the only non-French person given this accolade was Danny Kay (known as one of the great Epicureans).

Anyway, it is always presentation over substance. Mousse appears in nearly everything, fruit puréed to death with gelatine, wrapped in a thin sponge and glazed with more gelatinous coulis. One team I worked with created a lychee mousse – yuck! 'Mon Dieu' (formidable), the French would say.

And what about the vast amounts of solid chocolate they use for a display? Moulded, peeled and stacked up high – such a waste. But the proof is in the pudding, and often the taste is a let-down.

So, let's have perfection over complexity. A perfect Bakewell Tart with thin, crisp pastry, moist almond sponge and soft icing, or a Millefeuille, very crisp, feather pastry with soft vanilla pastry cream. "Run before you walk", Mother would say.

Get the basics right first!

Magic Hands Holgate

You can spot an artist straight away. Someone with a natural 'touch'. A natural culinary finesse is something that cannot be taught.

Back then, Chris was only nineteen and working in a team of five in the pastry kitchen of the *Bath Spa Hotel*. It was Forte's flagship, a 5-star luxury hotel overlooking the beautiful city.

Chris was struggling along amid the chaos of the busy, successful hotel. There was no leadership, the costs were out of control and the other 25 chefs were also running around like headless chickens. Often, Chris would be there until 2:00am finishing off the Danish pastries and croissants for the morning breakfast rush.

Eight chefs were gone within a week and I spent time with Chris. "Forget the croissants Chris, they're French anyway, concentrate on the bread". Within a year, we were making 500 loaves and 2,500 rolls a week. The favourites were the Three Cheese and Onion, Black Olive and Rosemary, and Sweet Basil. Once on the right course, he flourished and honed his skills to such a high level. We prepared dinners with Marco and Raymond, but Chris would outshine them all.

It was Chris's pastry work that was so impressive. His chocolate work was magical; identical chocolate cups and saucers filled with iced coffee parfait, fudge squares as the sugar cubes and biscuit shaped teaspoons, often for banquets of 100 or more.

His cakes were equally as good; the sponges moist, even and well balanced in flavour. Whether it was a 'Thomas the Tank Engine' cake to an almost exact replica, a four-tiered wedding cake encased in handmade chocolate cigarettes or even pulled sugar paint brushes for wood grain biscuit palettes – everything was to such a high standard. Ice cream, sorbets, parfait, petits fours, mousses, soufflés, gâteaux, tortes, and strudels… all came out consistently perfect.

On one occasion, Chris made a two-dimensional replica of the American Museum to take to New York. Somehow it made it there intact and it adorned a huge opera gâteau I made there. The New Yorkers were amazed (overdoing the praise as you'd expect) and they could not believe a teenager had made the pièce montée.

After seven years, we both moved on and have lost touch over the decades. I bet he's in the good old USA earning a fortune now, and rightly so!

Scrumping Time

Near Ilminster in Somerset, my parents would often take me to Perry's Cider Farm each year. 'The Home of 'Scrumpy', that's the proper Cider. The smell alone would make you tipsy. Apples were everywhere either being stored, pressed or graded. We would taste the various ciders in shot glasses, then make up a blend to be distilled in our own flagons. It was dangerous stuff mind, one glass and you were flying!

The humble English Apple, the envy of the world, is a fruit we love dearly. Who would argue for a better dish than the simple Apple Crumble? The 'Bramley' is my favourite, of course, as it is high in pectin and is so versatile. Other classic dishes include Tarte Tatin, 'Kuchens', Charlottes, Flans and the famous Apple Strudel.

In 1974, I was a mere lad and I began a career working under German and Austrian Chefs. My Dad and I worked evenings and weekends in a busy restaurant.

Here are a few tips for making a crumble:

- The apples (Bramleys if possible) need to be cooked. No water, just a little lemon juice and sugar to your taste added to the cut up apples.
- Use a thick bottom pan with a lid on a medium heat. Remove the lid once it has boiled, stir and cook out but not to a purée. Then cool and keep chilled.
- For the crumble, the basic ratio is 2:1:1 (flour: sugar: butter). For an 8-10" dish, you will need 300g of plain flour, 150g of caster or demerara sugar and 150g of soft unsalted butter. Put all these ingredients together in a bowl and just rub between the fingers to form a breadcrumb texture.
- You can experiment with the crumble by playing with the ingredients. For example, use half granary/half plain flour or a third ground and flaked almonds, a third plain, and a third wholemeal flour. Substitute honey for some of the sugar. Use half dark soft brown sugar. Margarine is also a fine alternative to butter. Plus, you can add seeds, oats and nuts to give your crumble an edge.

A Tart Tart

The French call it 'Tarte Tatin' – very romantic. We call it an upside-down apple flan, but hey ho, each to their own! And, of course, we have Bramleys – in my opinion, these are the best apples for cooking.

Ingredients

- 300-400g of Caster Sugar
- 8-10 large Bramley apples
- 250g of Unsalted Butter
- 1 packet of Puff Pastry
- Apricot Jam (for the glaze)

Method

1. You'll need a large non-stick frying pan. Remove the handle. Strew a generous amount of sugar (say 300-400g) over the base. Peel 8-10 large Bramleys, then quarter and remove the score with a paring knife.
2. Arrange the apple segments around the pan, filling in all the gaps with smaller pieces, if necessary, cram them in! Slice half a packet of unsalted butter (250g) and bury in between the apples.
3. Place on a good flame for up to 30 minutes. The sugar and butter will become caramel. Turn often to ensure an even colouring. Leave to cool and refrigerate (overnight if required).
4. Roll out a packet of puff pastry to just cover the pan. Docker (prick with a fork) well to ensure an even rise. Lay on the apples and trim. Rest for 10 minutes so the pastry does not shrink when cooked.
5. Bake in a hot oven at 180-190°C fan for 30-40 minutes. Lower the temperature halfway through if the pastry is too coloured. Make sure the pastry is well cooked. Leave to cool right down again.
6. To turn out, warm the pan again over a flame and gently shake until the tart moves. Place a board or plate on top and then carefully turn upside down.
7. Glaze with some boiled and sieved diluted apricot jam.
8. Serve with ice cream and/or cream 'Chantilly'.

What a lovely Pear!

Conference, Williams, Bartlett, Anjou, Asian, Concorde and the gorgeous Commice. Pears were my Dad's favourite fruit. That delicate perfumed flavour that is so useful in many dishes. Mulled, stewed, crumbled, poached or even grated in a salad. Try mixing them with apples in a pie – amazing! The most famous dish from classical cuisine is Poire belle Hélène, (named after the composer Jacques Offenbach), the alternative to Peach Melba. It is a 'Coupe' dish filled with vanilla ice cream, poached pear and dark chocolate sauce, decorated with rolled wafer biscuits. Another classic favourite is venison loin with pears poached in red wine.

Here is a recipe for the classic Pear and Almond Tart:

Take 3 or 4 pears of your choice, peel and take out the core at the base using a melon baller. Place in a saucepan, add a little lemon juice, a cup of sugar, a cup of water and some vanilla essence. Place on a lid and boil, then simmer slowly until soft (20 minutes or so depending on the ripeness of the pears). Leave to cool in the syrup.

Make or buy an 8"cooked tart case.

Ingredients for the filing:

- 2 Medium Eggs (should weigh approx. 100g)
- 100g of Unsalted butter or Margarine
- 100g of Caster sugar
- 75g of Ground Almonds
- 25g of Self-Raising Flour
- 3-4 cooked Pears (cut into 8 segments)
- A little Almond Essence
- 2 dessert spoons of Apricot Jam
- Flaked Almonds (to sprinkle)
- Icing (to decorate)

Method

1. Mix the eggs, butter, sugar, ground almonds, flour and essence together into a mixing bowl and whisk/beat to a smooth batter.
2. Spatula the mix evenly into the tart case. Lay on the pear slices in a circle.
3. Sprinkle with flaked almonds and set to bake at 150-160°C (fan) for 30-40 minutes.
4. When cooked, leave to cool. Meanwhile, boil the apricot jam with the same quantity of syrup from the pears. Strain and reduce to a thick consistency.
5. Using a brush (a new 1" paint brush is best), glaze the whole tart.
6. To finish, pipe on a criss-cross thread of white icing.
7. Alternatively, add slices of poached pear and whole raspberries, then seal with a sugar glaze.

The Ritz in Paris

Roger
Roger, le Dodger

"Oui Chef, pardon". I had just dropped a teaspoon on the marble slab – too much noise!

Monsieur Roger was a class act. "Cook with style to produce stylish food," he said. He cooked on an 18th century copper stove that had been updated to gas. The Welsh dresser was full of designer china, some with his distinguished 'S' scrolled in the centre. All in the open kitchen of his Flemish 2-star restaurant *'Scholterhof' (Robin Hood)*.

Roger had an aura and gravitas that enabled him to get away with anything. The restaurant was very tasteful with award-winning gardens that attracted high society. He was known as the 'Spoon Chef' (the first utensil invented) and would cater for canapé parties where all the food was served in spoons. I loved it!

After I had worked a 'stage' with him back in the late 80s, he invited me to an event in Paris. I flew in from Chicago not sure what I was letting myself in for, so took as much cash as I could – knowing Roger! We stayed at *The Ritz* (of course!) and it began there with a wine tasting reception. Château Latour in Magnums back to 1968 – the second most revered claret to Château Petrus – with foie gras and truffles en croute to wash it down. Wow! 'This was good' I thought.

"Let's eat at *Jamin*", Roger says. Joël Robuchon's most famous restaurant that was booked up a year in advance. "I will phone Joël". That night, we ate an amazing meal. Raviolis, Tête de Porc, Îles Flotanttes etc. Then onto the *Crazy Horses* nightclub – Roger had an eye for the 'dames'.

The next evening was the big event, a Toque Blanc dinner at the *Taillevant* restaurant. I was the only Brit and muddled along with my pigeon French while eating the 'pigeoneau'. I was on a table with Bocuse, Verge and Lenotre. In my twenties, this was a moment to savour, the most famous chefs in the world and I was having dinner with them talking about all things food. Roger was off somewhere charming all the ladies. I spotted little Raymond Blanc in the distance, but I was with the top guys.

Next day, back to the USA to cook burgers, Surf-n-Turf and all things American.

I returned to 'Blighty' shortly afterwards and worked on the opening of a beautiful country hotel in Ascot. Roger came over with Madame Roux and had dinner. I tried my hardest to impress him with a 7-course meal. The only course he raved about was the original Francis Coulston's Sticky Toffee Pudding. You see, we do know our puddings over here in the UK. Is there anything better than a good Bakewell Tart or a proper 'heavy-on-the-nutmeg' Custard Tart?

Christmas Tips

The golden rule in any professional kitchen is 'mise-en-place' – pre-preparation. Everything prepared before a meal (the veg, gravy, warm plates, serving cutlery, sauce-boats, carving knives, utensils and so on). Preparation is the name of the game.

The Bird

If you really want to cook a whole bird, remember that turkeys, capons and chicken should be cooked on their sides (so the breast does not dry out), whereas duck and geese are cooked on their backs. If you chose to cook just a large turkey breast wrapped in foil, a good guide is to cook at 140°C (fan oven) for 1 hour and 40 minutes.

In most professional kitchens, we cook the turkey breasts separately; the legs are boned and stuffed, most butchers will do this for free! Cook the turkey legs (boned and rolled) the day before. This will ensure they are cooked, give you the bones for the stock and all the lovely cooking juices for the gravy. Rosemary is also the most suitable herb to season turkey.

Cranberry Sauce

So easy to make and you can actually make this a week before! Put fresh cranberries in a thick bottom pan and add sugar, orange zest and juice. Boil with the lid on and then leave to cool – simple!

Vegetables

Do not leave these to the last minute. Pre-cook the green veg in rapidly boiling, lightly salted water and refresh several times until thoroughly cold. Store and reheat with seasoning and butter.

Roasties

Only season when they come straight out of the oven. The salt destroys the oil and will make them stick to the tray. Try a little celery salt for extra zest.

Goose fat is expensive. Try making your own by cooking duck legs in oil (confit), and have duck for dinner in November. Keep all the fat from the roasting tin and store in the fridge – this will be great for crispy roast potatoes on Christmas Day.

Meringues

You should use granulated sugar, not caster sugar. Try adding a handful of chopped roasted hazelnuts before cooking. This is called 'Japonaise'. Meringues cook for 1 hour at 100°C.

Stuffing

Traditionally, there are two stuffing's served with goose (sausage forcemeat and a bread farce).

The Mince Pie

Secret mince pie pastry: 450g of plain flour, 300g of pastry margarine or unsalted butter (at room temp), 150g of icing sugar and 2 egg yolks.

Just go ahead and work hard to a smooth dough, cling wrap and chill for at least 2 hours. Don't forget the golden rule of resting before baking to stop shrinkage.

The Pudding

Add brandy just before serving the brandy sauce, it tends to lose its flavour if added too early.

To flame a pudding: At the last-minute fill a ladle (metal) up to a half full with brandy (or Grand Marnier/whiskey/rum), place over a small gas flame, warm a little and tilt the ladle to set the alcohol alight. Pour over the pudding and dim the lights. Please be careful to ensure the pudding dish is deep!

The Gravy

The 'fond de cuisine'. A good gravy/jus/espanole/estouffade/demi-glace takes precedence when it comes to a good roast dinner. Most menus use the word 'jus' which actually means juice. Jus-Lié is the correct term of a thickened gravy using the cooking juices from a joint. Anyway, I'm waffling!

Here is a good basic espanole which can be made days earlier:

Ingredients

- 2 large Onions
- 1 Leek
- 2 Carrots
- 2 Celery Sticks
- A pinch of Salt (for seasoning)
- 1 whole tube of Tomato Purée
- 2 tablespoons of Plain Flour
- Half a bottle of good Red Wine
- Gravy Browning
- Mixed Herbs (for seasoning)
- 1 litre of Beef Stock

Method

1. Take aromatic vegetables (2 onions with skins, 1 leek, 2 carrots, and 2 celery sticks) and wash. No need to peel, just roughly chop up and start to fry with a little oil in your largest pan.
2. Season with salt and stir continuously until they have a nice colour and start to release their flavours.
3. Add 1 tube of tomato purée and a sprinkling of mixed herbs.
4. Cook out the tomato mixture for 2-5 minutes then add two tablespoons of plain flour, and cook yet again for a further 2-5 minutes, stirring occasionally.
5. Add half a bottle of good red wine. Boil, then add 1 litre of good, cold beef stock.
6. Bring to the boil and using a ladle, take off the foam/scum as the sauce boils. This is imperative as the impurities will go back into the sauce making it bitter and cloudy.
7. Turn down the heat a bit to a 'ticking boil', remove more foam/scum as it appears. Add a little gravy browning if required.
8. Then strain and stir whilst cooling to stop a skin forming. Correct the sauce by reducing, adding a little-diluted cornflour if too thin.
9. Add all the juices from the cooled cooked turkey, re-boil and reduce until you achieve the desired thickness.
10. The fat separates when cold and the 'Marmite' left at the bottom of the bowl is the flavour you want.

You must be baking mad!

"That's rubbish, you don't do it like that". I'm shouting at the TV from the comfort of my microcoil mattress. Contestants have been told to slice a warm fatless sheet sponge in half to make a Tiramisu. Impossible, the sponge will just tear. Or, piping hot Italian meringue onto ice cream for a Baked Alaska (the ice cream should be covered with a thin layer of sponge macerated with a liqueur like Grand Marnier).

Why are there so many food cookery programmes on the TV? There was a cake maker cutting thick regal icing with a knife (wrong – a scraper is required), then it should be 'polished' smooth with the excess icing. Instead, it was all cracked and uneven. My Dad would be turning in his grave.

You need to ensure that you leave enough time to make the cake so it can be 'fed' with brandy over the next couple of months. This recipe makes an 8" round cake.

Ingredients

- 100g of Unsalted Butter,
- 100ml of Vegetable Oil
- 100g of Caster Sugar
- 100g of Dark Soft Brown Sugar
- 4 Medium Eggs
- 100g of Self-Raising Flour
- 100g of Plain Flour
- 2 teaspoons of Cocoa Powder
- 1 teaspoon of Treacle
- A cap of Vanilla Essence/Almond Essence/Bun Spice/Rum/Brandy – to taste)
- 1kg of Mixed Fruit with Peel (this can include Dried Cranberries/Figs etc.). Douse with a generous amount of Rum/Brandy
- 50g of Glacé Cherries – halved
- 50g of Nibbed Almonds

Method

1. Beat the butter, oil and sugars together until creamy.
2. Add the eggs and mix in well. Sieve in the flours and cocoa powder and then mix to make a thick batter.
3. Add in the treacle and flavourings (essences). Stir and finally, add the cherries and nuts. Keep tasting and adjust the spices accordingly.
4. Place the mixture into a well-buttered and greaseproof lined cake tin (ensure the paper is a couple of inches higher than the tin). Smooth over the top with a wet hand or spoon.
5. Bake at 130°C (yes a low temp) for at least 2 ½ hours. Test with a metal needle in the centre.
6. Remove from the oven, place on a rack and cool. After 20 minutes, turn onto a cake board that has been brushed with brandy. Leave overnight to cool with the tin still on.

To store, remove the tin and place the cake and board in a shopping bag, 'feed' by pouring on brandy, wrap and store in a cool place (i.e. larder). Repeat the feeding each week.

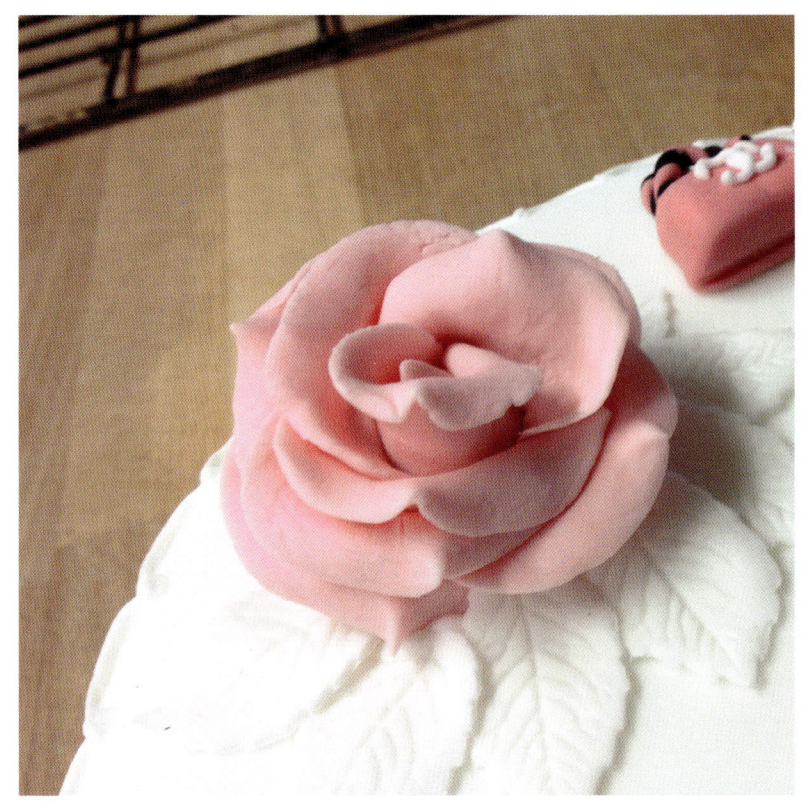

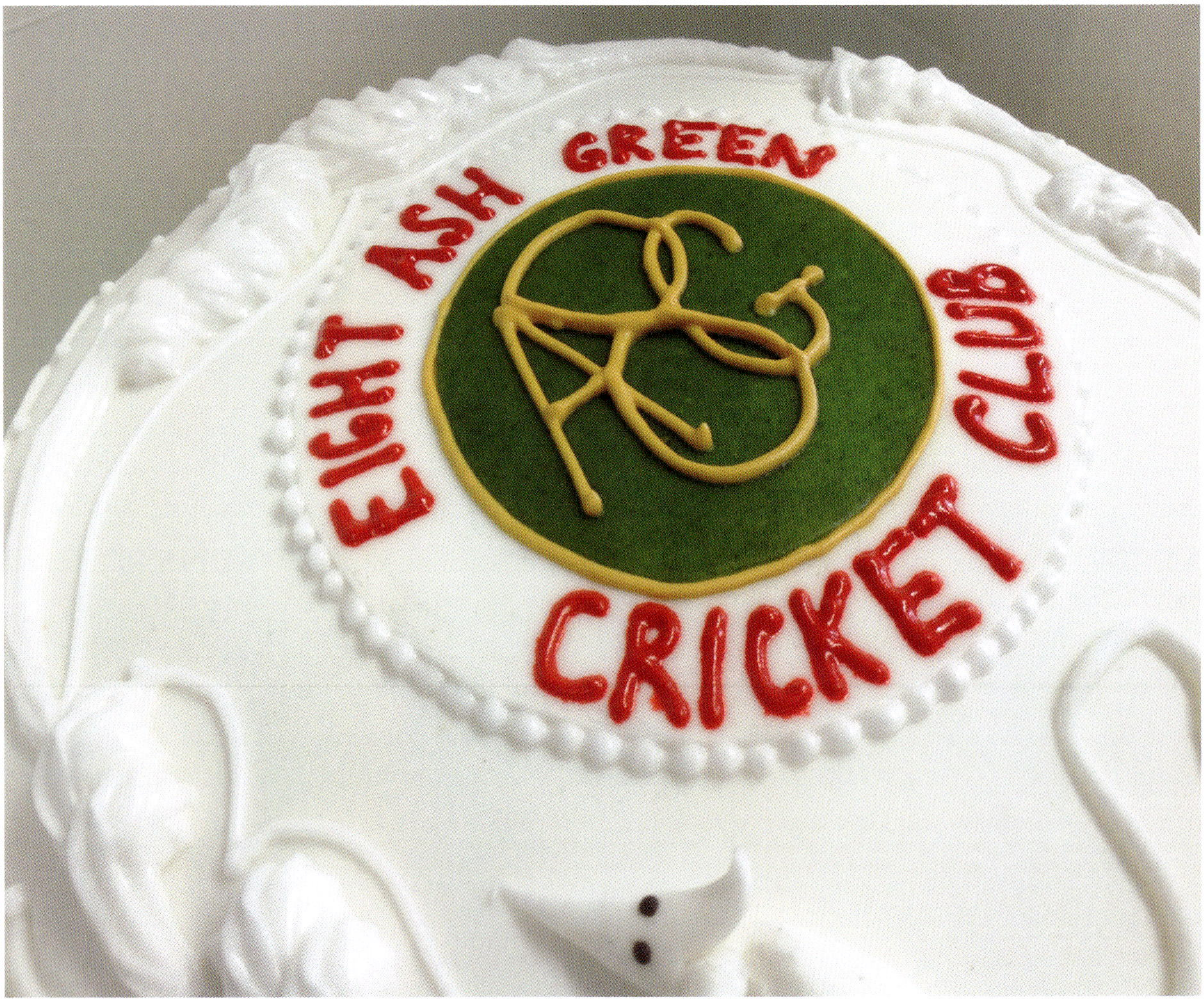
EIGHT ASH GREEN
CRICKET CLUB

Icing a Cake

Icing a cake can seem like a daunting project. This is an easy way to guide you through the process.

Ingredients:
- For an 8 inch cake, use 1/2 a jar of sieved Apricot Jam
- A cup of Water
- Marzipan (you will need a 1/3 of the cake weight – around 500g depending on how thick you like it!)
- A splash of either Brandy/Rum or Whiskey
- A dusting of Icing Sugar

Utensils:
- Two 2 inch Paint Brushes
- Saucepan
- Rolling Pin
- Icing Sugar Dredger
- Palette Knife
- Smoothers and Crimpers

Here is the Regal Method:

1. For an 8 inch cake, boil 1/2 a jar of sieved apricot jam with a cup of water and reduce to a syrup consistency. This will make it easy to brush over the fruitcake and prevent it from going mouldy. Cover the cake completely with the hot jam using a brush and wipe off the excess straight away. Put a little booze (brandy/rum/whiskey) on the board before placing on the fruitcake. This adds flavour and again, stops it going mouldy!

2. Roll out the marzipan (you will need a 1/3 of the cake weight, around 500g) using icing sugar on the table and pin. Make sure it does not stick to the table. 5mm is about the thickness you want. Allow extra to be sure there is enough to cover the whole cake. Lay on the cake and let it naturally find its way, creases will appear on both round and square cakes. Gently, without pulling, push the marzipan into place using the base of your hands.

3. DO NOT use a knife to trim the edges. Use a scraper or pallet knife. Cut downwards in line with the sides of the cake. Using icing sugar on your hand, rub over the cake to smooth the finish. You can buy smoothers, which are just plastic trowels that are good for squaring the sides and top. Then go and make a nice cup of tea!

4. Now comes the icing. Take the same amount as marzipan and mould with your hand until smooth, then press and flatten to a thick disc. Dust the table with icing sugar, place on the icing, dust the rolling pin and start to roll out SLOWLY, turning after EVERY press. Use more icing sugar if the icing starts to get tacky or sticky.

5. When your icing is evenly rolled out to the same thickness as the marzipan, make sure it is freely moveable. Take the cake and pour 2 bottle caps of your preferred tipple over the marzipan and brush all over. This makes the icing stick.

6. Carefully lift the icing by rolling up over the pin. Lay over the cake and repeat for the marzipan. This time, after the trimming, polish the icing using the leftovers. Mould the spare icing together, flatten in the palm of your hand and lightly rub all over the cake. Blemishes and marks will simply disappear and the icing will shine.

7. If you have a crimper, now is the time to make your indented pattern. It is best to let the icing dry for a day if you are going to use strong colours in cut-outs or piping as the colour may bleed.

8. Have fun decorating. If you are using cut-outs, roll the icing very thinly and stick onto the cake with a little water.

Simple Mince Pies

Festive Feasting Mince Pies

Back in 1972, I was merely fourteen years old. This restaurant I worked for was very famous in Essex back then. I started work at 10:00am (my first day), washing up and attending to all those other kitchen porter duties. It was brilliant, such a great, busy atmosphere with controlled hectic organisation. The heat, noise, staff speaking (swearing!) in Italian, German and French, made it an alive and 'happening' place to be. Dad was in the larder knocking up Black Forests, Strudels, Prawn Cocktails and huge bowls of salads. The vast amounts of washing up never seem to end. I remember getting paid quadruple time – £2.00 an hour. (£12.00 for six hours work). I thought I was the richest man in town!

Since then, I have worked over the festive period until my 40s, mostly as the chef of 5-star hotels, putting on elaborate banquets for wealthy guests who expect to be overindulged. How they ate all the food amazes me still! The welcoming Christmas Eve Gala Dinner, Midnight 'Figgy Pudding' on return from Mass, the Christmas Day Breakfast, Lunch (four-courses), Afternoon Tea with the Queen's Speech, the Evening Buffet, Boxing Day Brunch, Pre-Panto Lunch and lastly, the Gourmet Banquet (six-course). Still hungry? If the gluttony of food didn't kill you, the alcohol would!

A great mince pie is topped with a Viennese biscuit. This biscuit recipe was co-designed by my one of my previous apprentices.

Ingredients

- 250g of Unsalted Butter,
- 125g of Icing sugar
- 1 Egg
- 150g of Plain Flour
- 100g of Self-Raising Flour
- 1/2 a cap of Vanilla Essence
- Half a Glacé Cherry or some Flaked Almonds
- Icing Sugar (for dusting)

Method for the Viennese Topping

1. Cream the butter and sugar together in a mixing bowl.
2. Then add 1/2 a cap of vanilla essence, egg and both the plain and self-raising flour into the mixture.
3. Using a 'star nozzle', pipe a rosette on the top ensuring all the surface is covered.
4. Preheat the oven at 170°C.
5. Then add half a glacé cherry or some flaked almonds, if required.
6. Bake in the oven at 170°C for 15-20 minutes.
7. When the Viennese biscuits are cool, dust with lots of icing sugar.

Festive Feasting Continued...

- **Cooking steaks:** Leave out of the fridge to get to room temperature. Use olive oil (not extra virgin) as it has the highest 'burn' temperature. Season the meat first, except for kidney and liver.
- **Using garlic:** Always try to use fresh, not processed. There is no need to chop or crush the garlic too finely. My favourite method is to roast the whole bulbs with the meat (lamb/beef), then squeeze out the purée.
- **Best potatoes:** Keep peeled potatoes in water and add a slice of old bread.
- **The creamiest mash potato:** Boil the spuds in their skins until almost cooked. Drain, then cool a little and peel. In a large pan, boil milk and cream, add the potatoes (sliced) and continue to cook until soft. Finally, purée with a masher and whisk.

Cigar Chocolate Truffles

Chocolate Truffles

(Ideal for Christmas presents or stockings)

A little too much chocolate is just about right. Go on, indulge yourself and others by having a go at making these chocolate truffles.

Ingredients

- 350ml of Double or Whipping Cream
- 300g of Dark Chocolate (couverture)
- 200g of Milk Chocolate
- Icing Sugar (for dusting)
- 700g of Dark Chocolate/Milk Chocolate or White Chocolate (whichever is your favourite!)

Method

1. Boil 350ml of cream (double or whipping) in a saucepan on the hob.
2. Remove from the heat and add 300g of chopped dark chocolate (couverture) and 200g of milk chocolate.
3. Stir with a spatula until smooth; pour into a plastic tray and leave to cool – then refrigerate overnight to set. Scoop out a tennis ball size piece of mix onto the table/marble slab, and heavily dust with icing sugar.
4. Dust your hand as well and roll into a long sausage, using more sugar if necessary. Try to touch the chocolate as little as possible.
5. Now, take off pieces and ball up onto a tray. Place 700g of either dark, milk or white chocolate in a plastic or glass bowl and melt in the microwave for only 40 seconds. Stir, then heat in the microwave for another 30 seconds. Repeat until melted.
6. Leave the chocolate to cool, stirring as often as possible until cool to touch. This is a quick version of tempering.
7. Finally, dip each truffle in the melted chocolate using a fork and place on silicone paper.
8. Then leave to set and decorate.

Bermuda Tea

There's something unique about the lemons that are grown in the 365 Virgin Islands of Bermuda. They are large, juicy and have an amazing, perfumed fragrance. Wonderful scents and aromas are carried in the air from the beautiful flowers.

It sure is a hot place to work, the temperature reached 90°F along with sweltering humidity. The sea breeze just wafted warm air around. We would have to change our paper chef's hats at least four times and change our jackets at least once in a shift. There was a lot of chaffing going on! Hence those long shorts everyone wears out there!

The only relief was the tea. You wanted to put your head in the urn to cool off. A large bucket of tea was made every couple of hours so the kitchen staff could just ladle a glassful for themselves at any time. There is no precise recipe, but we all made it and it was the lemons that just made it so refreshingly thirst-quenching.

I make it here and often give it to regular customers in summer. Our summers are only going to get hotter thanks to climate change so have a go:

Ingredients
- 20 Teabags (any type of English Breakfast Tea will do)
- 2 pints of Water (to boil)
- 1lb of Caster Sugar (est. 454g)
- 6 large Lemons
- 1 whole packet of Ice (crush this)

Method
1. Place around 20 tea bags in a large metal bowl.
2. Boil 2 pints of water in a pan on the hob.
3. Add the 2 pints of boiled water to the 20 tea bags, then stir once and quickly remove the tea bags (you do not want to get the tannic taste of tea – just the flavour).
4. Pour in up to a pound of caster sugar and stir.
5. Now, add the juice of 6 large lemons, throw in the used lemon halves as well for extra flavour.
6. Shovel in a whole packet of crushed/flaked/beaten ice and stir with a large ladle.
7. Leave for 5-10 minutes.
8. Decant into a tall glass and drink through a straw (paper if possible).

At the end of the shift, it was 'strip off our work clothes and dive in the sea' as our hotel jutted out into the bay. Then it was a quick change, a short moped ride to the beach bar. It was 'stuff the tea' and 'bring on the Rum Swizzles!'

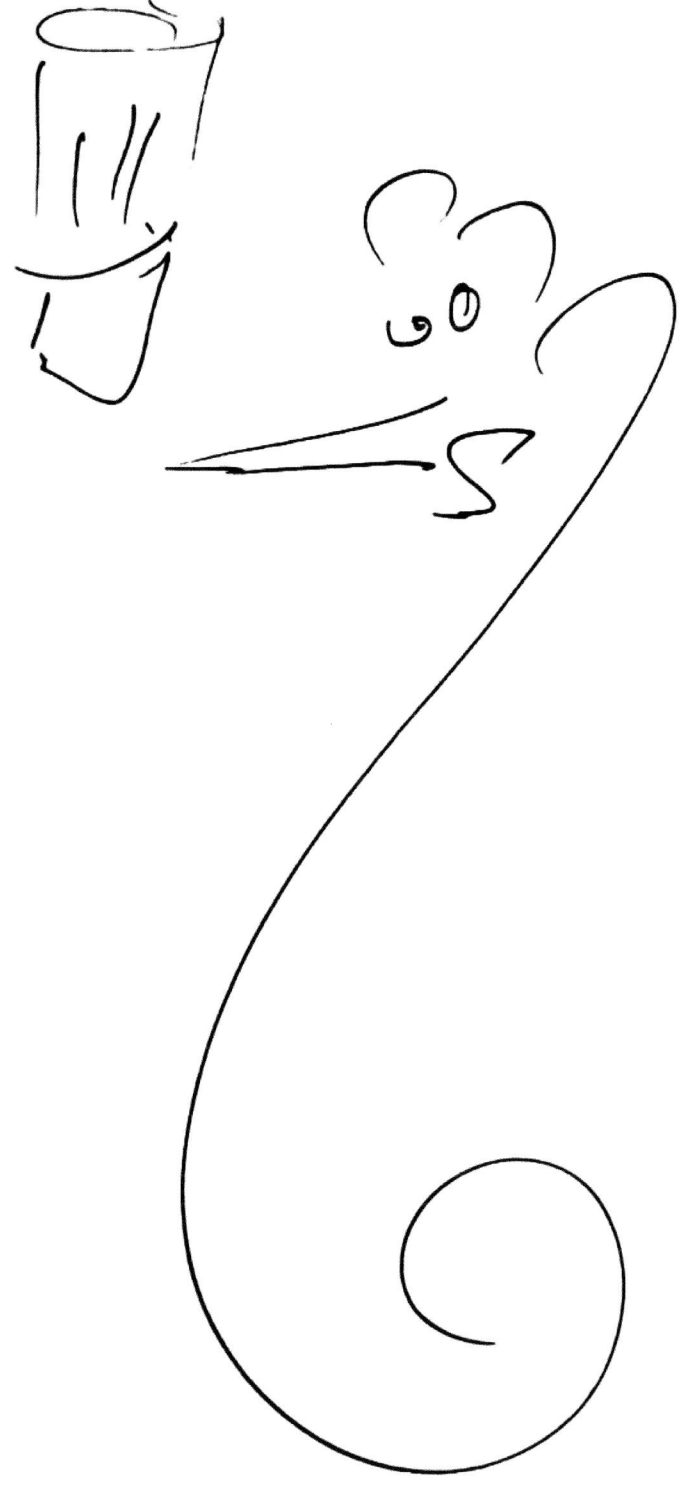